Regatta Sailing

PER SKJØNBERG
Regatta Sailing

Translated by R I Christopherson

Technical Advisor: Michael Richardson

Illustrations: Jacob Hochlin
and Michael Richardson

Adlard Coles Limited   London

Granada Publishing Limited
First published in Great Britain 1972 by Adlard Coles Limited
Frogmore, St Albans, Hertfordshire AL2 2NF and
3 Upper James Street, London WIR 4BP

Copyright © 1969 Per Skjønberg
First published in Norway 1969 by Utgitt av Norsk Seileskole
This translation copyright © 1972 Adlard Coles Limited
Second Impression 1973

ISBN 0 229 98664 1

Filmset by Keyspools Limited, Golborne, Lancashire
Printed in Great Britain by
C. Tinling & Co. Ltd, Prescot and London

Contents

Training Programme

In order to obtain good results in yacht racing, it is essential to draw up a long-term training programme, and it is important to train regularly.

The basis of all training must be to understand what happens to the boat, its sails, the wind and the current while we are actually sailing. Without this basis of knowledge we shall be marking time; we shall never derive full benefit from our special training programme and our competitive sailing.

This book should tell you all you need to know if you want to win your races. It is written for the young sailor, and for those sailors who are always young at heart. But first and foremost it provides a basis for good teamwork, since it makes available to all the knowledge and experience necessary to get a boat first across the line.

Get a friend with a similar boat to train with you. Discuss together the problems as they arise, and exchange your ideas and experiences. Read the book, ask your club instructor, if you have one, and help your rivals. Make a note of your experiences and observations.

The main thing is not to win, but to want to win.

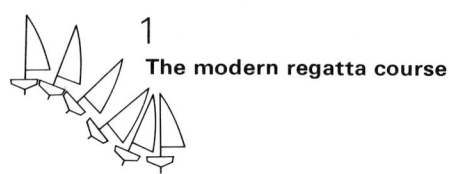

1

The modern regatta course

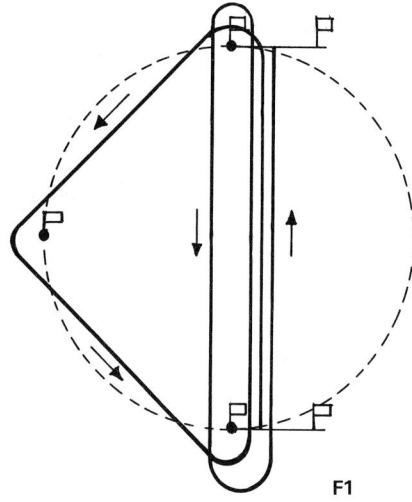

The regatta course of today is a triangle inscribed in a circle. The actual course is marked by buoys, and has its longer side parallel to the direction of the wind (the windward and running legs), and the other two sides (the reaching legs) set at an angle of 45 degrees to it. F1

F1

Olympic course. Diameter $1\frac{1}{2}$ and 2 nautical miles

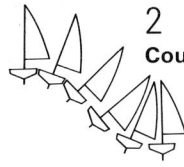

2

Courses sailed in relation to the wind on the Olympic course

If we divide a circle into 360 degrees, then we can imagine that boats are racing on a compass rose. Navigating on a course with the aid of a compass like this will eventually come quite naturally. The compass shows the number of degrees steered by the boat in relation to the wind when tacking, reaching and running, in order to round the marker buoys. F2

To windward
1 Dead to windward (in irons)
2 Pinching
3 Hard on the wind
4 Close reach
5 Beam reach

Off the wind
6 Reach
7 Broad reach
8 Run
9 Dead run

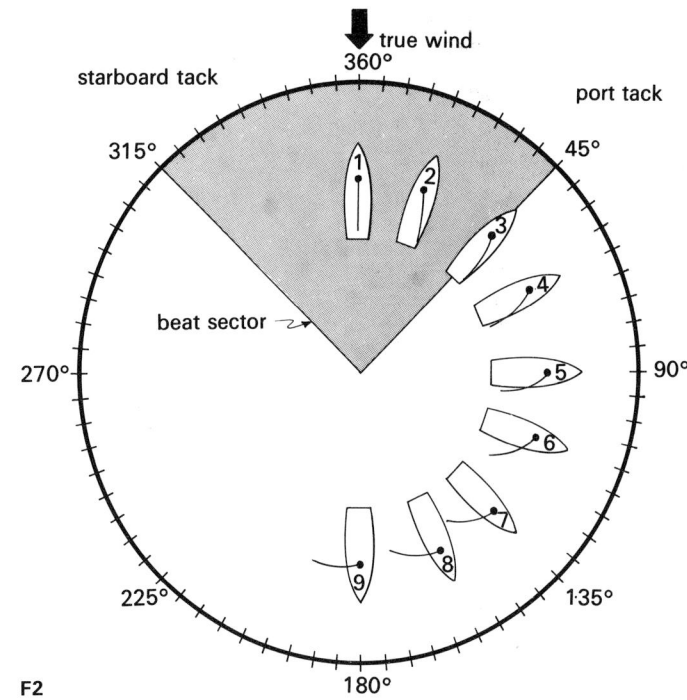

F2

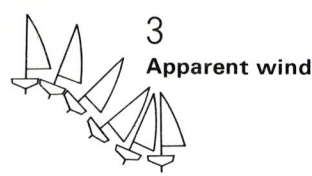

3
Apparent wind

The apparent wind is the wind that blows on your sails, and the flag or wind indicator at your masthead shows you its direction. This is composed of the meteorological or true wind (as shown by a flag on the shore or on a marker buoy), and the wind created by the speed of the boat.

When beating against the wind, there is an angle of about 15 degrees from the meteorological wind to the sailing wind, and 45 degrees to the course steered by the boat. As we alter course into or away from the wind, the apparent wind will change its direction, and with an increase in speed on any given course the apparent wind draws more ahead.

A wind indicator is one of the most important items of equipment on board. At all times it indicates the direction of the apparent wind, and enables one to steer the boat and trim the sails correctly. F3, F18

apparent wind
true wind   0°   15°
boat's course
45°
wind indicator

F3

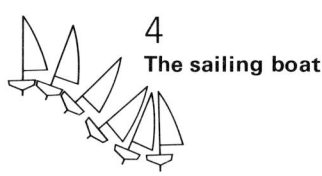

4
The sailing boat

A boat's sailing qualities are almost entirely dependent on its design, and it takes a long time to become completely familiar with them. It is important to realise the qualities required in a hull if it is to perform well under sail. F4

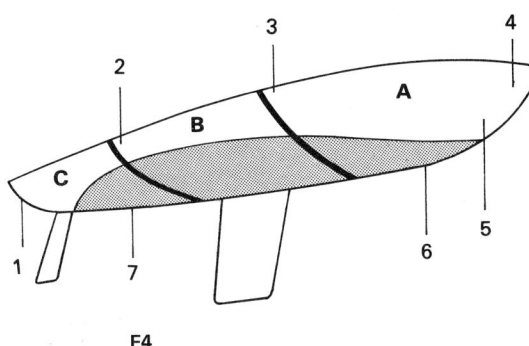

F4

The bow section A meets the water and the waves, and should have the following qualities: the bow should cleave the waves, and prevent the boat from pitching into the seas and losing speed and rhythm. Under the waterline the entry of the hull must provide sufficient buoyancy to enable the boat to rise above the water and encourage early planing. The bows must also have considerable reserve buoyancy, to resist the tendency of the sails to depress the bow when sailing before the wind.

The midships section B must bear the weight of the boat and crew, and provide sufficient stability to counteract the heeling moment when under sail. Maximum beam should be at the point where the crew are positioned when sailing to windward, to gain greatest benefit from their sitting-out power.

The stern section C should harmonise with the lines of the bow to ensure that the boat is easy to steer at speed and in a rough sea. It should also cause the flow of water moving round the hull to the transom to leave a wake with as little turbulence as possible.

Desirable features, found on modern dinghies, are as follows.
1 stern of reasonable width, to avoid lifting when heeled
2 flare amidships to increase the sitting-out power of the crew
3 flared topsides to deflect bow waves
4 low freeboard to reduce windage
5 fine bow for low resistance in waves
6 deep forefoot to reduce pounding in waves, provide dynamic lift for planing, and for reserve buoyancy to prevent nose-diving when running
7 long, flat run aft, allowing clean flow and reducing drag when planing.

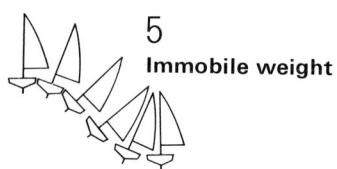

5
Immobile weight

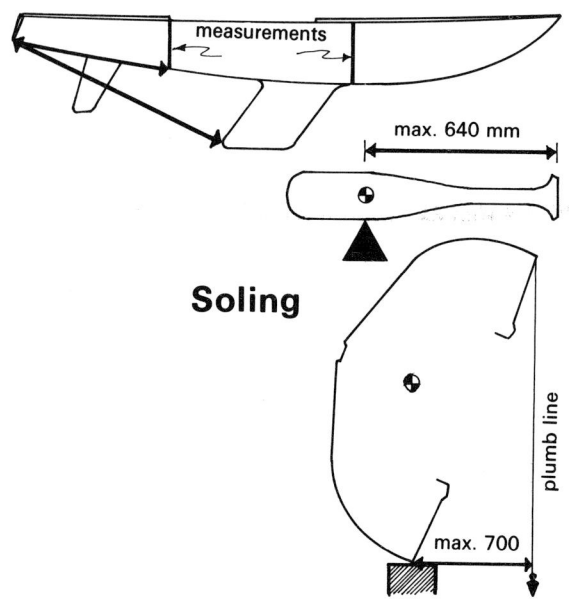

measurements

max. 640 mm

Soling

plumb line

max. 700

F5

Don't be fooled by the chap who says, 'A few pounds here and there won't make much difference.'

A good racing yacht should weigh as little as possible consistent with the rules of its particular class. In the Snipe class, the largest international class, 3 lbs over weight would be cause for concern, and the minimum weight for the class, don't forget, is 192 kg (about 420 lbs).

But the most important consideration of all is where the weight is placed in the hull. The rule is lightness above the waterline and as far up as possible; weight below the waterline and as far down as possible.

The deck should be light. Modern glass-fibre production makes it possible to a certain extent to distribute the weight in the hull in the desired proportions. The correct method is to make the bow, stern and deck of the boat as light as possible, so that the weight can be concentrated amidships and in the keel.

There is a very effective and simple way of checking the centre of gravity of the Norwegian-designed Olympic Soling class boat. The hull should be placed on its side, balancing on one gunwale. It should not cant over in the direction of the keel as long as the distance from the lower gunwale to a plumb line suspended from the opposite gunwale exceeds

700 mm (27$\frac{1}{2}$ in.). There is a similar method of checking the centre of gravity of the iron keel. This should be placed on a trestle: if the keel heels over to the left when the distance from the upper extremity of the keel to the balance point on the trestle exceeds 640 mm (25$\frac{1}{4}$ in.), the bottom of the keel is too heavy. F5

The weight, and weight distribution of the mast can be checked in the same way. It should be lightest at the top and heaviest at the foot.

A heavy mast with a light top is much better than a lighter mast with a heavy top. A boat with a topheavy mast is liable to yaw or roll in a rough sea.

All gear and fittings above the waterline should be as light as possible. Check *every* fitting systematically, replacing it if it is too heavy and doing away with it if it is superfluous. A racing Dragon might cut her weight down by about 100 kg (220 lbs) in this way. Make sure that the hull is particularly light in the bow and the stern.

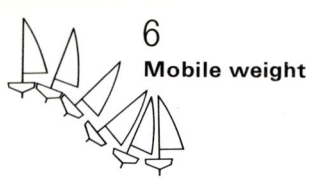

6
Mobile weight

Mobile weight means anything that can be moved while you are actually sailing—crew, sail bags, food and clothing, for example. Place all mobile weight amidships. Two incidents from international yacht racing illustrate this.

The American J-class *Ranger* was one of the fastest racing yachts ever built. She was over 130 ft long, had a displacement of 188 tons, and carried a crew of 25. In 1937 she was racing against *Endeavour I*, *Endeavour II*, *Yankee* and *Rainbow*.

They were hard on the wind, racing neck and neck, when the skipper of *Ranger*, Harold S. Vanderbilt, sent three of his crew forward to prepare a spinnaker. The sailing master, Roderick Stephens Jr, called out, 'They're going away from us!', whereupon Vanderbilt called his three crewmen back immediately.

As soon as these three, whose total weight was about 500 lbs, returned to their normal crewing stations amidships, the 188-ton *Ranger* once again surged past her rivals!

During the Skaw Race in 1967, on the leg from the Skaw to the Rakkebåene, *Heppe XV*, a 23 ft Norwegian offshore cruiser, had rounded the mark ahead of her Swedish rival. The latter, however, was coming up fast, and the skipper of *Heppe XV* told his two crewmen to lie down on the bunks in the cabin in order to increase the speed. This didn't help, but when they lay down on the sole of the cabin the Swede was fairly quickly outdistanced.

Concentrate weight amidships and as far down as possible, particularly in a dinghy.

The best way to observe the flow of water round a boat moving at sea is to stand on the deck of a passenger ship and watch the hull cleaving through the waves. You will observe a belt of water lying along the side of the ship and moving with it. This is the so-called inner layer. If we launch our boat in dirty water, particles of the water will be pulled along with the boat in such a way that the second water layer, the so-called laminar layer, slides up against the rough surface, producing turbulence. In order to produce as little friction as possible, the laminar layer should be as wide and long as possible. We can achieve this if the underwater part of our hull is perfectly smooth and even.

Grit, or a dent in the hull, makes the laminar layer turbulent. Surface un-evenness must be filled in or polished off.

A smooth hull is most important at the bow and forward part of the hull. The bow makes contact with the water and, if it is uneven, turbulence is started at this point. The result is that the entire

F6

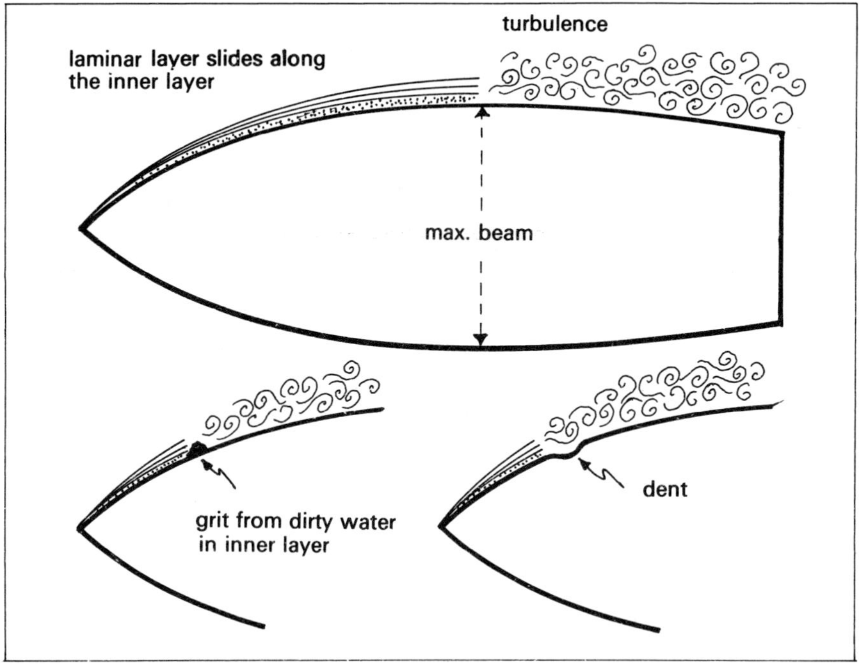

turbulence

laminar layer slides along the inner layer

max. beam

grit from dirty water in inner layer

dent

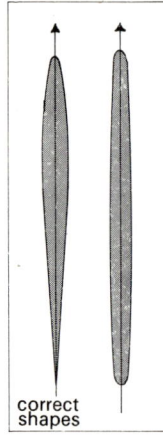

F7
Rudder and keel

correct
shapes

underwater portion of the hull produces turbulence, including the rudder and keel.

Turbulence generally begins at the point where the boat is broadest (beamiest). For this reason she should be sailed down by the bow in light airs. This will increase the distance from the bow to the point of maximum beam, and will extend the laminar layer further aft. In strong winds sail with the bow raised to reduced wetted surface, as well as to prevent nosediving.

When speed increases the laminar layer becomes thinner. Boats that plane at great speed, such as the Flying Dutchman and the Trapez, go through the water with a very thin laminar layer. Planing boats must have particularly smooth after sections, because when they are planing, the water makes its first contact with the area near the keel.

The transom should have clean-cut edges in order to ensure that the water flow is freely released. The water flow will adhere to a curved transom edge.

16

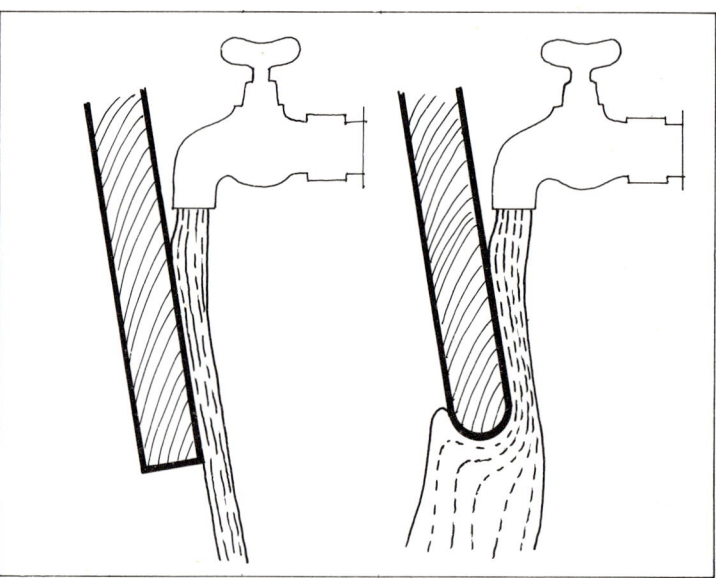

F8
Trailing transom edge shapes

8
Frictional resistance of air

The action of the wind on a sail is the same as that of water on a hull. The inner layer of air is at rest close to the sailcloth. Observe the dust on a car when the sun is shining. It will remain stationary, however fast you drive. One layer of air merely slides over another and, no matter how much you polish the paint, the dust will always stay put. The most important thing is to ensure that the surface is smooth and even. The cloth should be well finished, and must be carefully maintained to avoid creasing.

The crew present considerable air resistance. In light airs crew members should lie down, and should wear their life jackets under their jerseys. See that the weight is concentrated low down at one particular point, and maintain a small angle of heel.

Various racing dinghy and keel boat racers have experimented with masts on which ridges, fins, etc, have been placed as 'turbulence generators', intended to pull the air flow onto the mainsail's low-pressure side. This theoretical advantage is subject to debate and fashion.

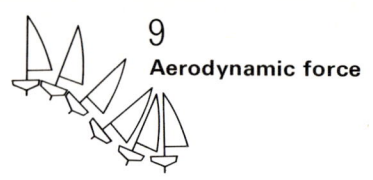

9
Aerodynamic force

Sailing is a very complicated and exacting sport presenting a wide range of problems. The helmsman who fails to realise exactly why his boat behaves as it does in various situations will soon find his rivals romping away from him.

Aerodynamic force is the result of a current of air striking the sail. *It always*

F9

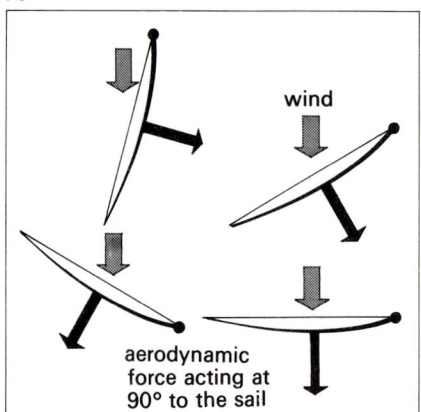

aerodynamic force acting at 90° to the sail

F10

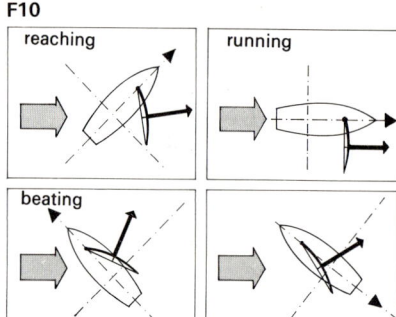

reaching · running

beating

F11

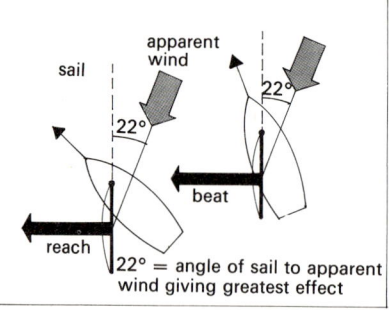

sail · apparent wind · 22° · 22° · beat · reach · 22° = angle of sail to apparent wind giving greatest effect

acts at an angle of 90 degrees to the sail, irrespective of the angle of incidence of the air stream. F9

When we set sails on a keel boat, the boat will sail in the direction in which the aerodynamic force works, modified by the lateral resistance of the hull and keel. Thus a boat can run, reach, beat and even sail backwards. F10

When the sail is at an angle of about 22 degrees to the apparent wind it achieves maximum aerodynamic force, and the boat will sail at top speed. F11

At this angle the air flow remains laminar over both sides of the sail, and the aerodynamic force results from high pressure on the windward side and low pressure on the lee side. The air current to windward of the sail accounts for about one-fifth, and the air current to leeward four-fifths, of the total aerodynamic force. F12

The sail will pull when the air strikes it at an angle of 10—22 degrees; it will

18

either stall or flap in the wind if we sheet it in or ease it out more in the air flow. When turbulence is created or increased, the power of the sail is reduced. The worst mistake is to sheet a sail in too hard. This will destroy four-fifths of its aerodynamic force. P1, F13

When on a broad reach, or running, the air flow becomes turbulent behind the leech, or in the shadow of the sail, and the drive caused by suction is reduced. However, although the aerodynamic force

F12

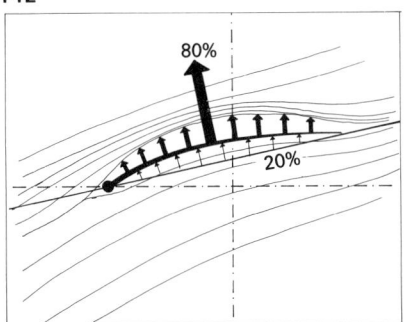

P1

The Killing class dinghy *Alice* beating with a jib which is pulling with a laminated air flow to windward and leeward. The mainsail, however, is stalling in the wind and creating turbulence to leeward because it has been sheeted in too hard (F13)

19

P2
Small lengths of yarn threaded through the sail show that the air flow passing over the lee side of an OK dinghy is perfectly laminar (F13)

F13

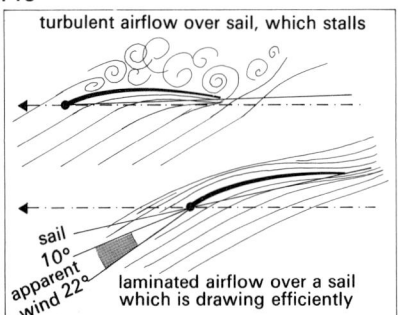

turbulent airflow over sail, which stalls

sail 10°
apparent wind 22°

laminated airflow over a sail which is drawing efficiently

F14

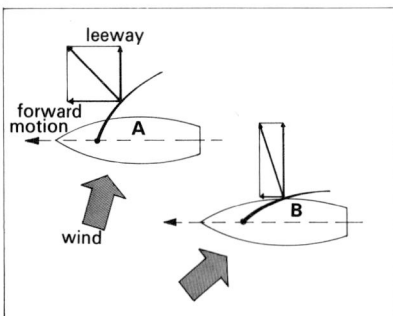

leeway

forward motion

A

wind

B

is less than when close-hauled, it is more effective as it becomes closer to the desired course, and less force is used against the lateral resistance of the hull, keel and rudder.

Even if a sailing boat were a round saucer without any keel or rudder, we should nevertheless be able to sail it by adjusting the aerodynamic force to the direction in which we wanted to proceed. The leeway course coincides with the aerodynamic force. In order to sail into or across the wind, the boat needs the lateral resistance of the hull and keel. The drift to leeward acts at right angles to the keel, and the forward motion of the boat acts parallel with the boat's longitudinal axis.

The forward motion of boat A, which is reaching, and of boat B, which is beating, is the resultant of the drift to leeward and the aerodynamic force of the sail. Always trim your sail in such a way that the aerodynamic force acts as much as possible in the direction of your course. F14

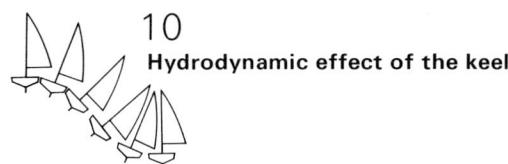

Hydrodynamic effect of the keel

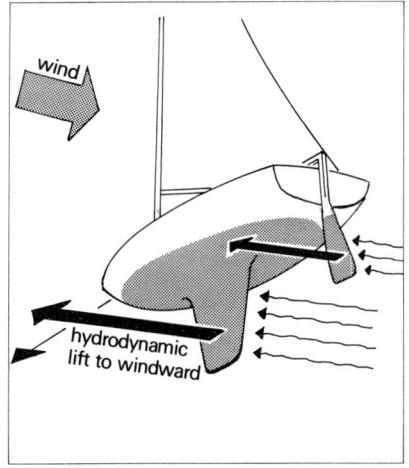

F15

keel and the rudder, a corresponding hydrodynamic force is created, pulling the keel in the water to windward. When these forces counteract one another, the boat is then sailing in perfect balance, with the least possible leeway. F15

In the upper drawing we see what happens when the boat is pinching and speed is reduced. The keel stalls in the water and turbulence is produced on the weather side. The boat's leeway increases to over 8 degrees. A keel and rudder stalling in the water reduce speed twice as much as a sail stalling in the wind! F16

When we sail fast the hydrodynamic force increases, and the amount of leeway is reduced. The keel shown in the lower drawing is on a boat sailing at full speed. The water flow is faster on the weather side. The hydrodynamic force increases, and leeway is only 4 degrees.

Always sail at full speed, with minimum heel, and with minimum movements of the tiller and minimum weather helm.

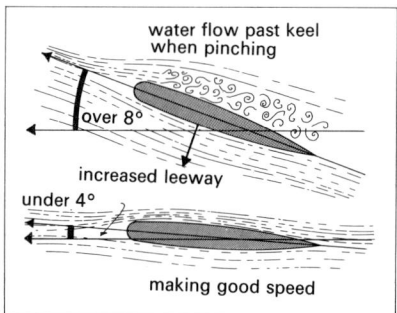

F16

The air flow over a sail and the flow of water round the keel and rudder act in the same way. On the leeward side of the sail an aerodynamic force pulls the sail up into the wind. To windward of the

11
Wind direction indicator

On the top of your mast you should fix a vane (an ordinary little burgee will do), which will turn with the wind. Beneath it mount two fixed arms, each at an angle of 30 degrees to the boat's longitudinal axis. When your boat is sailing fast, the vane or burgee will lie between the arms. F17

When you pinch and sail at reduced speed, the wind vane takes up a position outside the arms. F18

To get the wind vane to move forward, one must trim the sails correctly, bear away, and increase speed. If you steer closer to the wind the sails will stall still more, the apparent wind will be reduced and will approximate to the true wind, and the speed will be reduced. Finally, the wind vane will admittedly take up a position between the arms, but the boat will then be sailing so close to the wind that speed will be practically nil.

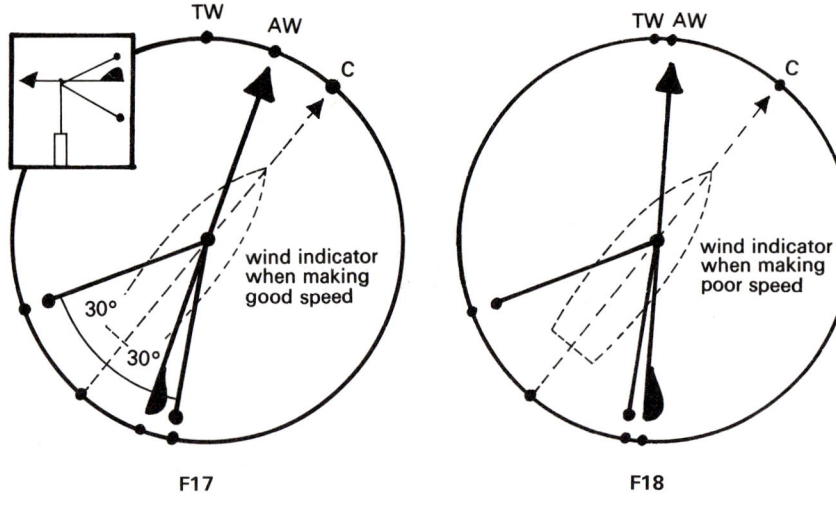

TW   AW
C
wind indicator when making good speed
30°
30°
F17

TW AW
C
wind indicator when making poor speed
F18

12
Beating at full speed

Helmsmen with a special flair for sailing 'by the seat of their pants' always sail their boats at full speed, with sails filled and with very little leeway, and generally get to the windward mark first.

We should sail in such a way that our boat gets to the spot at which the bows are pointing. We must in fact make good our direction to windward.

The apparent wind is constantly changing direction while we sail, shifting forward when the boat is moving fast, and abeam when we make the mistake of coming up too high into the wind and losing speed. It is essential to try to increase the boat's apparent wind speed! F19

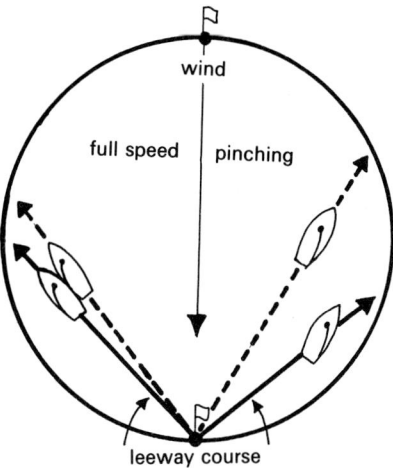

F19

Pinching: full speed to leeward

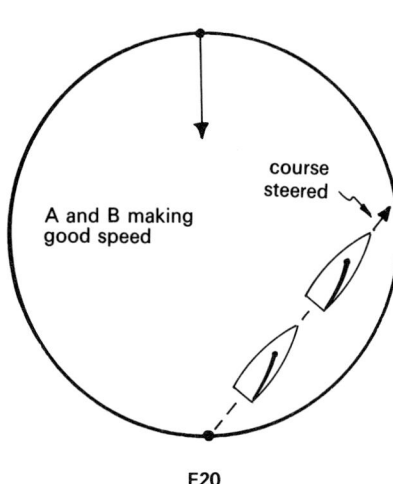

A and B making good speed

course steered

F20

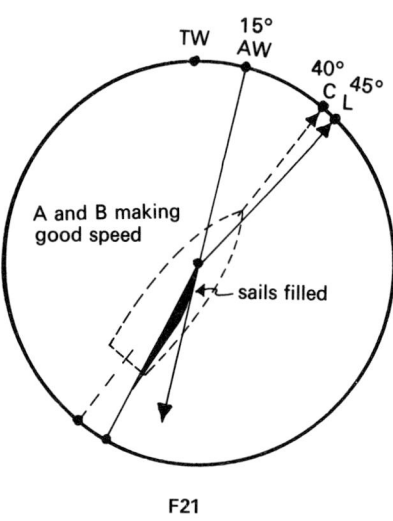

TW

15° AW

40° C 45° L

A and B making good speed

sails filled

F21

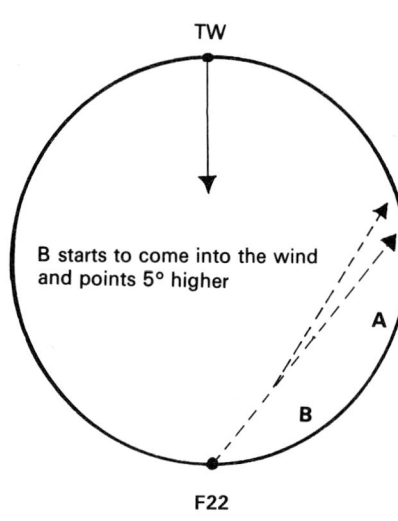

TW

B starts to come into the wind and points 5° higher

A

B

F22

It is very important to understand exactly what actually happens to the boat's course when we sail too close to the wind when beating. It is often very empting to sail a little closer to the wind in order to overtake a boat to windward when we are lying astern.

Example
You are helming boat B; I am helming boat A. The course steered by both boats is C, the leeway course L, the apparent wind and wind indicator AW, the true wind TW. We are both sailing at full speed. F20, F21

You decide to sail boat B 5 degrees closer to the wind in order to try to overtake to windward. As a result, the forward section of your mainsail is back-winded and the aerodynamic force is reduced. F22, F23

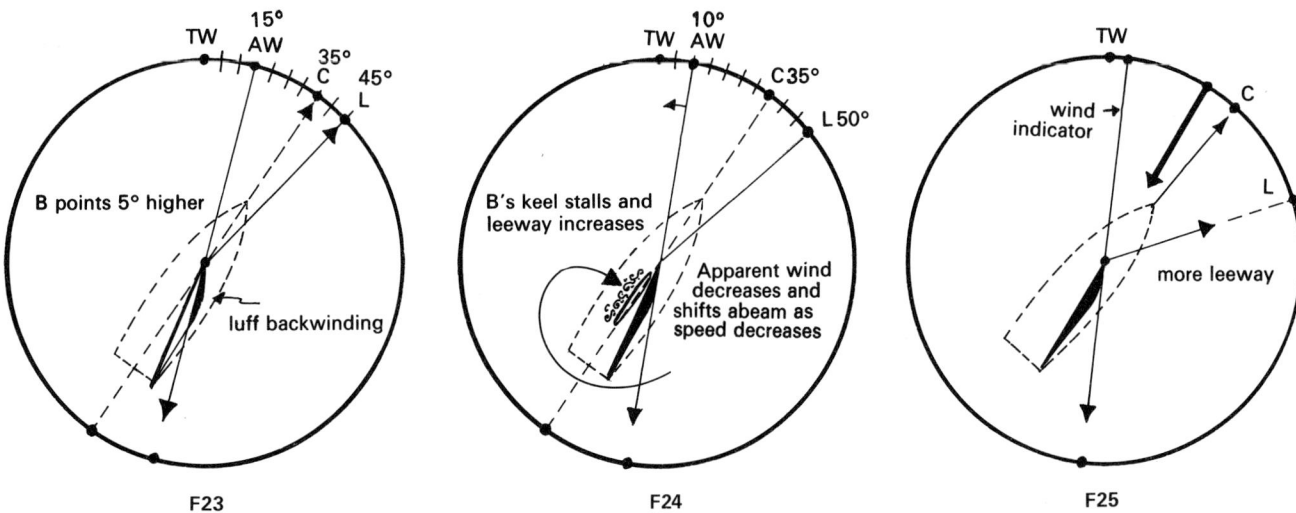

F23

F24

F25

After a few seconds your speed is reduced because your boat has started making leeway as the result of turbulence created on the windward side of your keel. The keel stalls in the water, and the hydrodynamic power is reduced. The boat's apparent wind speed is decreased.

The wind indicator veers in the direction of the true wind, and the sails fill once more. But leeway has been increased to 50 degrees. F24, F25

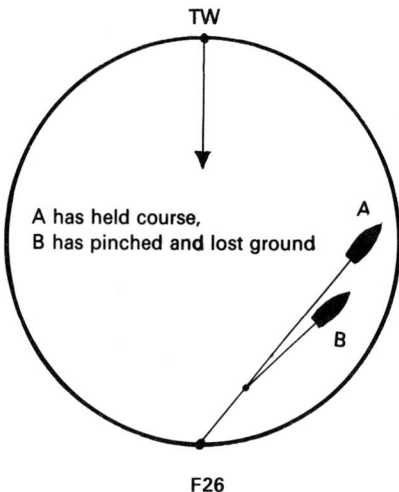

TW

A has held course,
B has pinched and lost ground

A

B

F26

You are now moving at full speed to leeward, and have achieved the very opposite of what you set out to achieve!

Correct course, sheeting and adjustment for maximum speed

Sailing in light winds:
sail flexibly with a fuller sail and twist,
have your sheets close inboard,
sheet your sails in lightly,
reduce friction by moving weight forward,
avoid pinching.
Result:
full speed to windward and normal amount of leeway.

Sailing in strong winds:
sail flexibly with a flatter sail without twist,
have your sheets well outboard,
sheet your sails hard down,
sail the boat upright,
reduce friction by moving weight aft,
steer less close to the wind.

P3

N 53 is beating with a large amount of leeway because the boat is pointing too high into the wind; the sheet is rove amidships instead of to leeward; the sheeting releases the leech, but does not flatten the sail. As a result the boat is heeling over excessively

Result:
great speed to windward with little leeway.

Once full speed has been reached, point higher into the wind and reduce the angle between the sail and the apparent wind.

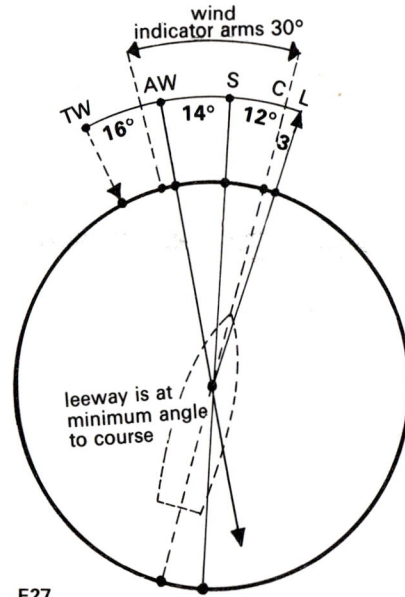

F27
The beating sector of a modern racing boat in a wind of about force 3. The true wind is TW, the apparent wind and burgee AW, the sail S, course steered C, leeway and drift L

The modern sail

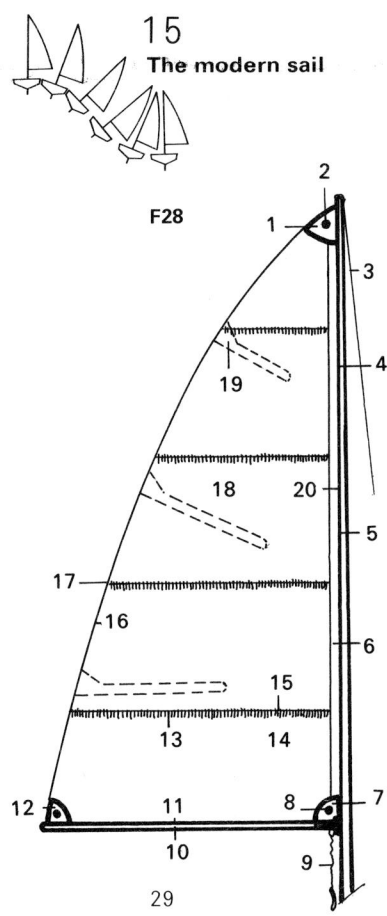

F28

1 Headboard
2 Head
3 Halyard
4 Boltrope
5 Mast
6 Tabling
7 Tack
8 Eyelet
9 Downhaul
10 Boom
11 Foot
12 Clew
13 Reef points
14 Belly
15 Reef band
16 Leech
17 Roach
18 Cloth
19 Batten
20 Luff

F29

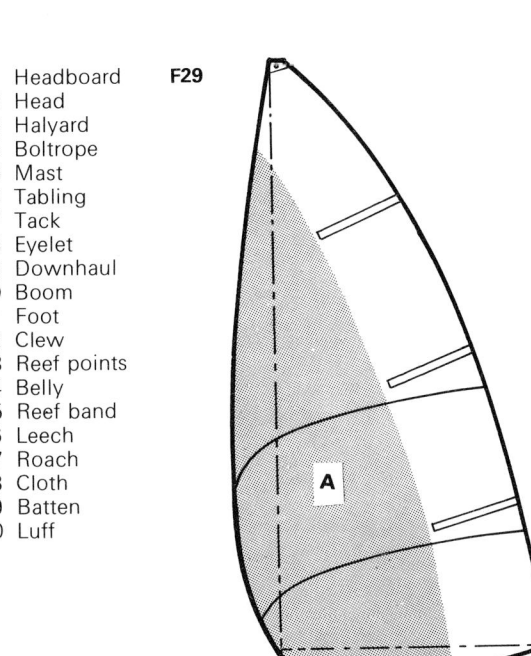

A modern mainsail has curved edges, and maximum area for use in running and reaching, and in light airs. Battens inserted into the leech help to keep the sail flat, as well as ensuring a clean air flow.

The shaded portion A is the part of the sail with which we sail when the leech is falling away in a strong wind. This part of the sail must never be allowed to lose its shape. F29

With a flexible mast and boom we can change the belly or draft of the sail. A straight mast and boom give the sail maximum draft (*a*), while a curved mast and boom give the sail a larger spread, making it wider and flatter (*b*). F30

Various forces are produced in the rig when a boat sails to windward (F31): (a) the load on the leech; (b) the pull of shrouds, forestay and mainsail luff; (c) the thrust of the sail, sheet and kicking strap; (d) the pull of the kicking strap; (e) the downward pull of the main sheet; (f) the forward thrust when the main sheet exerts a forward pull.

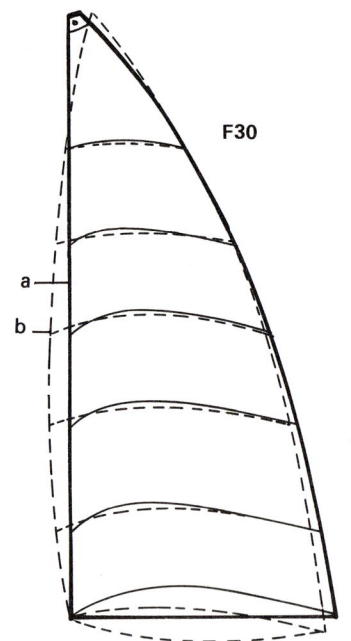

F30

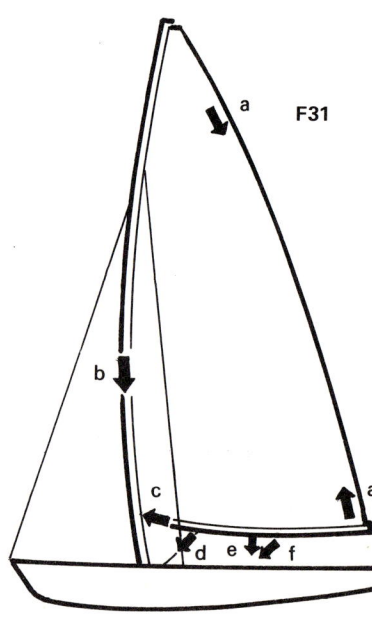

F31

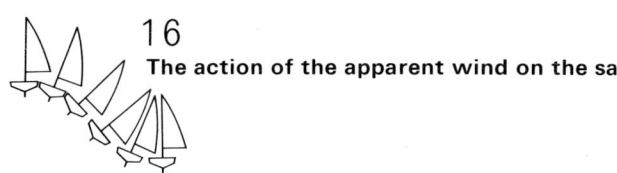

16

The action of the apparent wind on the sail

The apparent wind does not maintain the same direction and strength over the entire area of the sail. The true wind is strongest at the top, owing to frictional resistance at water level. The apparent wind tends to blow from a wider angle higher up the sail.

In order to maintain the laminar air flow we must, therefore, design and set the sail so that it subtends a larger angle with the longitudinal axis of the boat in its upper part. This is called giving the sail twist.

The sail should be sufficiently loose in the leech to automatically produce the right twist when the wind varies in strength and direction. F32, P4

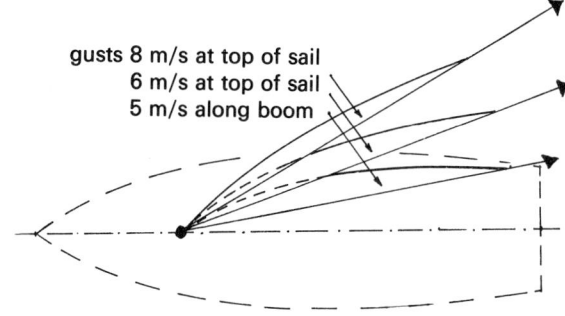

gusts 8 m/s at top of sail
6 m/s at top of sail
5 m/s along boom

F32

The direction and strength of the apparent wind acting on the sail when close-hauled in squalls

P4

Peder Lunde (Olympic FD gold medallist, 1960) and Per Ola Wiken sailing their Star *Sirene* with a correct twist in the sail, in a breeze at Saltsjöbaden in 1968. Note Per Ola's effective weight distribution, and Peder's correct position at the helm, enabling him to keep an eye on wind, weather and sails

Acapulco breeze was sometimes 2 metres per second in the troughs and 4 metres per second on the crests. When wind increases over crests, the air flow from the genoa is deflected onto the lower portion of the mainsail if it is too full along the boom. F34

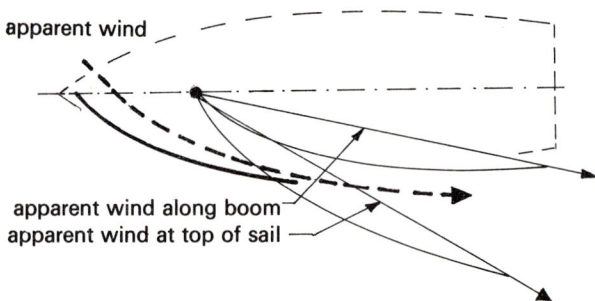

apparent wind

apparent wind along boom
apparent wind at top of sail

P5
Correct twist in the mainsail in a medium-force breeze. The boom has been sheeted so that the air flow from the jib does not strike the lower portion of the mainsail. Star *Sirene* in the Olympic races at Acapulco, 1968

F33
A genoa jib influences the flow of the apparent wind, causing the air current to move inwards towards the longitudinal axis of the boat over the lower portion of the mainsail

angle of apparent wind
at top of mast 20°
4 m/s   full sail

along boom 15°
2 m/s   flatter sail

Plate 6 shows *Sirene* at the bottom of a trough in Acapulco. The dotted line edging the sun shadow shows that the wind is being deflected onto the lower part of the sail. The boat has just sailed down the windward side of a swell at great speed. In the trough it encounters a reduced true wind, the jib is back-winded, and it in turn backwinds the mainsail.

The upper part of the mainsail is more effective in such conditions, because the wind is stronger and more even higher up. P6 shows a sail correctly set for light airs with a slight twist which enables the top of the sail to hold the wind. P6, F34

F34
When a mainsail designed for light airs and swell is set with a genoa it should be flatter along the boom and fuller near the top

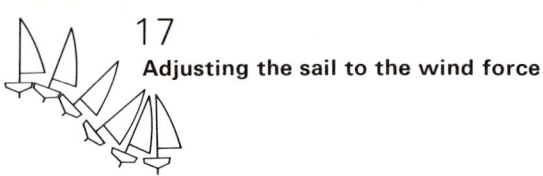
A well-known American sailmaker once said that after he had packed up a sail and handed it to the customer it would be ruined unless the sailor realised how to use it under full control.

Paul Elvstrøm's *Trapez*, in common with other modern dinghies, has a highly developed mainsail which can be used over almost the entire Beaufort scale, from light airs to gale force winds. It has draft intended for use in running, reaching and for special light weather conditions. How far should we flatten it when the wind really starts to blow? P7

In light airs and breezes the maximum draft of the sail may be as much as 10 per cent of the length of the foot; in wind strengths in excess of this, it may be 5 per cent.

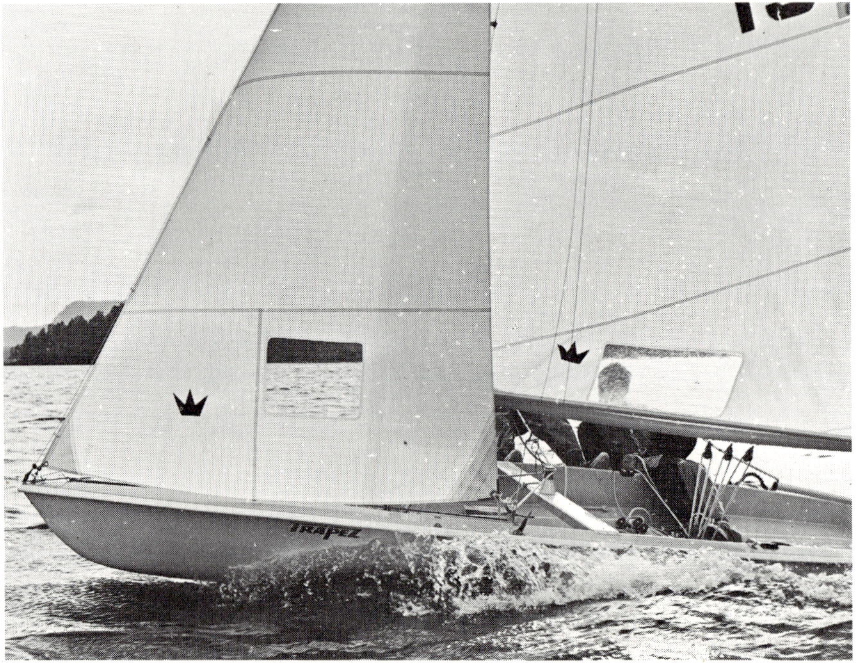

P8

This sail will be effective for reaching

P9

Sail for use in force 3 winds

P10

This sail is shaped for beating in light airs

P11

Sail sheeted in as for use in a fresh breeze

1 Up-end your dinghy on land, stretch a length of elastic across the sail on a straight mast, and measure the depth.

2 Attach a check mark on the sail with tape and stretch the elastic from the top of the mast to the foot of the sail. Give a slight bend to the mast by tightening the kicking strap.

3 Bend the mast until the elastic runs across the check mark.

4 Bend the mast and the boom, using the kicking strap and the sheet, until the elastic passes on the other side of the check mark.

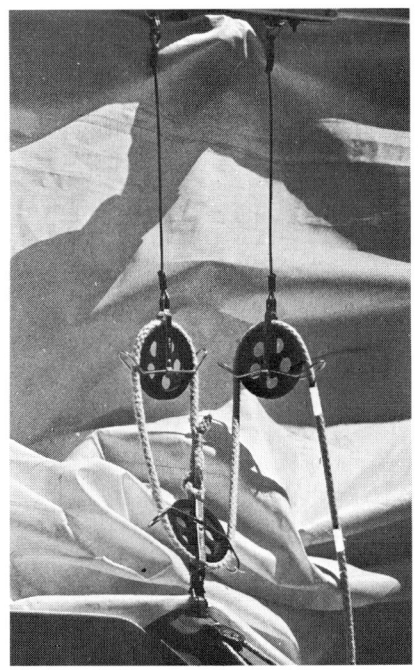

5 Launch your boat and try her paces against a rival boat. Leave the elastic in position. Your check mark will help you to regulate the bend in the mast. Put a mark on the downhaul and the mainsheet (P12) when your boat is sailing at full speed, and use these marks for reference for any further trimming you have to do.

Bend the lower portion of the mast, giving the sail at the dotted line the shapes shown in F35. The letters link the sail curvature with the mast curvatures shown in F41, shape A being produced when the mast is in position A, and so on.

P12

P13
Lay your sails on the deck or a clean floor in smooth even folds; place them carefully in the sail bag

F35

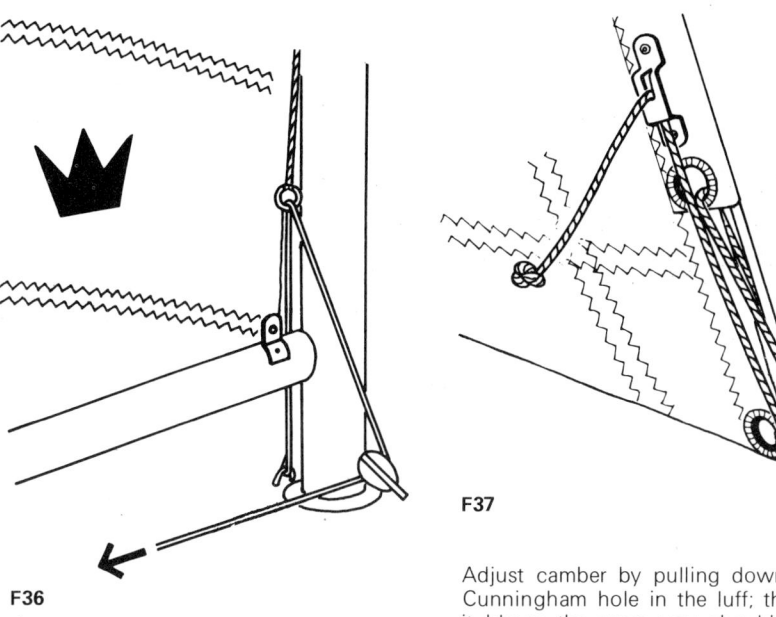

F36

F37

Adjust camber by pulling down on the Cunningham hole in the luff; the harder it blows the more you should take up on it. The purchase may be arranged in various ways. F36, F37

The shape of the jib and mainsail in a strong breeze. The line has been hauled tight, and the belly is well forward in the sail. The after part of the sail is slack and flat. F38

F38

The shape of the jib and mainsail in a light breeze, with the line slacked off, and the belly closer to the centre of the sail. The after part of the sail closes and holds the wind. F39

F39

Bend the top of the mast in order to slacken the leech: (*a*) for running and reaching; (*b*) for beating to windward in a force 3 wind; (*c*) beating to windward in force 4–5; (*d*) beating to windward in a strong breeze. F40, F41

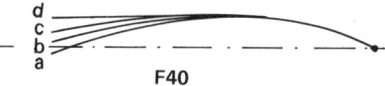

d
c
b
a

F40

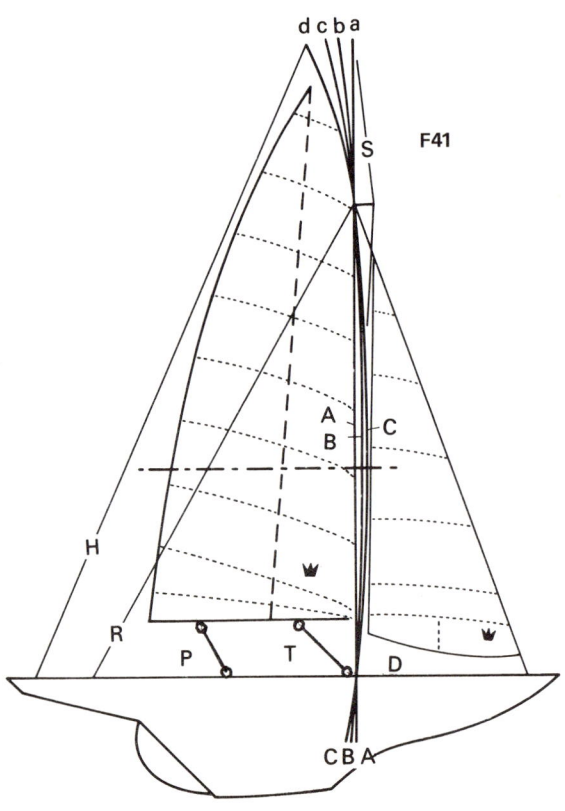

F41

The lower section of the mast is bent by moving the mast step aft and taking up on the backstay. The mast is straightened by moving the mast step forward, so that the forward edge of the mast bears against the deck. When the mast is stepped on deck the same effect can be achieved by taking up on the kicking strap T, and running the mainsheet P forward to a block or cleat. F41

In the Folkboat and Soling, the jibstay is tightened when taking up on the backstay H. The top of the mast can be adjusted by regulating the jumper stay S. In a Dragon or 5.5 metre, the jibstay can be tightened with the aid of the running backstay R. F41

The various adjustable parts of a rig, which vary with class rules and individual boats, and such devices as Cunningham holes, zips and stretch luffs on the sails themselves, enable the crew to alter mast bend, mast rake and sail shape over the different areas of the sails. These are designed or varied to suit wind force, the weight and hence the inertia of the boat,

P14
Jack Knights and David Hunt tuning their Tempest at Poole

Photo: Michael Richardson

the wave conditions and the angle of the sail to the wind.

Most Tempests until this time had been fitted with diamonds for mast control, whereas this mast is controlled by single swept-back spreaders set very high to control the topmast. The bend in the lower part of the mast is controlled by a powerful ram at the deck which is well eased in this photo to free the mainsail leech and help the boat to drive through the short seas. P14

Note the sail setting: no taut or slack leeches, perfect slot between jib and mainsail, perfect twist in the upper portion of the sail, great dynamic force directed forward because the sail is sheeted down to leeward, correct positioning of weight and helmsman, and leech parallel to the longitudinal axis of the boat, enabling it to make good speed to windward. P15

John Oakley in *Elusive* at the Soling World Championships in 1970

Photo: Michael Richardson

Setting the sails to suit the wind

The surest method of testing whether a sail is correctly trimmed to the wind is to thread a number of lengths of black wool yarn through the sail about 6–8 in. from the luff. This is the method used by experts such as Austin Farrar, best-known British aerodynamicist and sail maker. P2

A sail drawing properly, with a laminar air stream on both sides. The lengths of yarn on both sides are blown horizontally. F42

A sail with a disturbed air current to leeward. The lengths of yarn to windward are horizontal, while the strips to leeward are blowing up and down. The sail has been sheeted in too close to the longitudinal axis. This is the commonest fault and also the worst. F43

A sail which is stalling because it has been eased out too far. The result is that the leeward lengths of yarn are horizontal, while those to windward are blowing up and down. F44

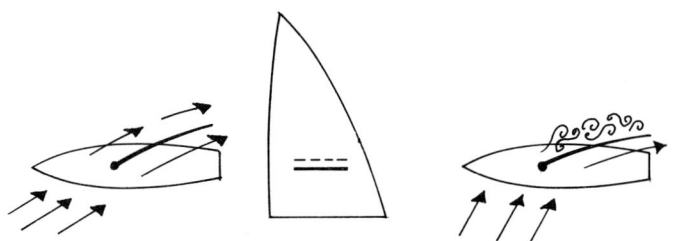

F42

F43

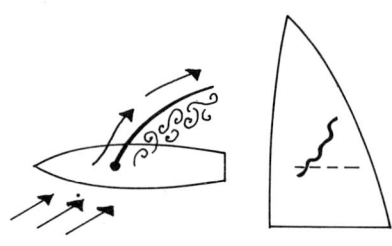

F44

P16

P17

A streamlined, easily driven boat, like the Yngling or the Soling, is easier to sail fast with flatter sails. A heavier boat, like the Dragon, with broad bows that offer more resistance, needs fuller sails to move at speed.

Flatter sails are best in light winds in smooth water. This enables the helmsman to point higher when sailing to windward, without losing speed. P16

Beating in a strong breeze and a rough sea calls for full sails, with a slack leech, especially in the upper section of the mainsail. P17

Sailing in light winds and a swell calls for a full sail, particularly in the upper half of the main. The leech must retain the wind and be trimmed loosely in order to respond to the constant changes in the strength and direction of the wind. P6

In strong squally winds over a smooth sea, flat sails with a slack leech are best, particularly in the upper part of the main. P18

HM King Constantine sailing his Dragon at Hankø with a specially sewn suit of Elvstrøm sails. The seams prevent the sails stretching, while the mainsail calls for a straight stiff mast

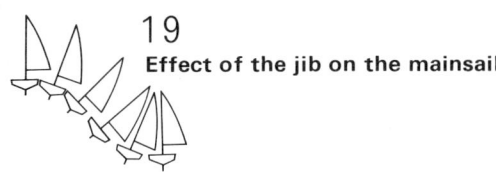

19
Effect of the jib on the mainsail

A genoa alters the direction of the air stream passing over that portion of the mainsail struck by wind from the genoa. It is very difficult to prevent this air stream from striking the luff of the mainsail. The lower two-thirds of the mainsail should be shaped to take the best advantage of this current of air.

On the Flying Dutchman, owing to the speeds attained, it is necessary to place the greatest depth of the sails closer to the middle. The genoa is the most important sail on the Flying Dutchman and must be carefully designed. It is important to ensure that the fullness of the mainsail is well aft and low down, in order to reduce the backwinding effect of the air current from the genoa. The Lofterød brothers in *Tine* in a swell and strong breeze. F45, P19

F45

Correct sail design on a FD

P19

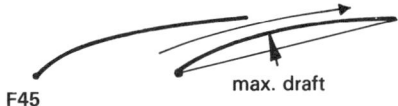

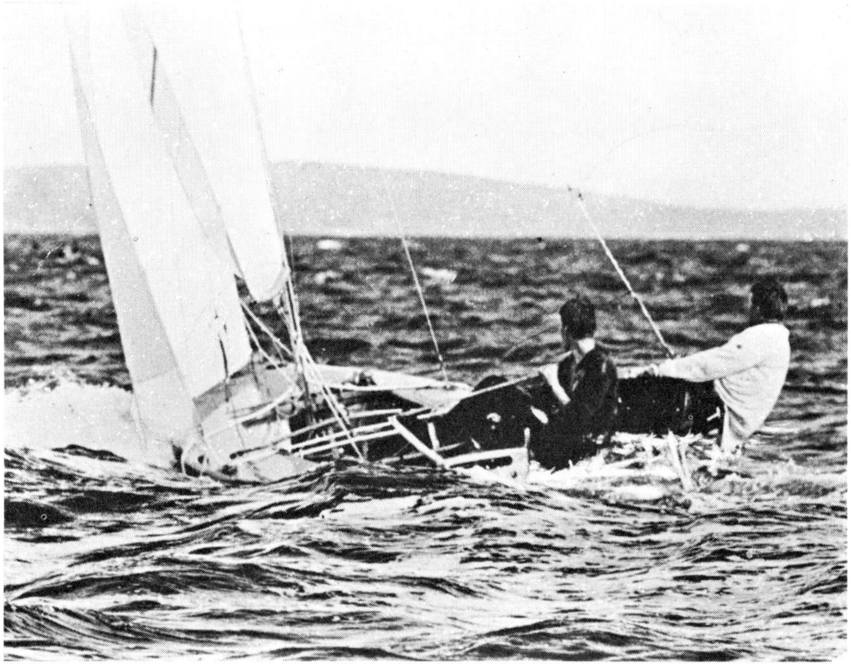

P20 The author with his son

The air current from the jib of a Snipe does not have the same effect on the mainsail as on a FD, because the greatest area of the jib works below the boom. Both sails operate independently in the air current, and are equally effective. But the slot between them must be of constant width, especially higher up. Maximum fullness should be well forward in both sails. The wetted surface of the centreboard is reduced in light airs because it rises out of the water when beating to windward. The mast is raked further aft to prevent the pull on the sheet and the weight of the boom from tautening the leech. The rake of the mast also tautens the luff of the jib. The foot of the main is horizontal, ensuring a laminar air flow over the lowest portion of the sail. The boat is heeling sufficiently for the sails to fill correctly. P20, F46

max. draft

F46

Correct sail design on a Snipe

The jib increases the air current in the lee of the mainsail. F47

F47

Jib sheeted in too hard. Unduly narrow slot. The air current is turbulent. F48

F48

The jib sheet eased out too much. No increase in the speed of the air stream. F49

F49

For examples of good adjustment of sails, see P14 and P15.

Set your jib sheet lead further forward
1 in order to increase jib fullness near the deck
2 in order to tighten the leech.

Set your jib sheet lead further aft
1 in order to make the top of the sail fuller
2 in order to slacken the leech.

Set your jib sheet further inboard
1 in order to sail higher into the wind
2 in order to increase the slot wind in lighter airs.

Set your jib sheet lead further to leeward
1 in order to increase speed and reduce heeling in stronger breezes and winds.

Main points to remember
1 A slack leech does not interfere with the slot air flow.
2 Sheet your jib in as far as possible in order to maximise the slot air flow.
3 Always sail with a jib which has its tack at deck level to prevent the air current escaping below the sail and producing turbulence.

20
Sailing with a flexible (bendy) mast

In a modern sailing boat the mainsail is the most difficult sail to adjust. The mast should be sufficiently flexible to enable the sail to be adjusted for all wind strengths.

Aluminium and glassfibre masts are the most suitable, because they retain their powers of recovery much longer than wooden masts. An aluminium mast that is too stiff can be made flexible by making small incisions in the track in the region marked X. Many class rules, however, do prohibit this technique. F50

The great curve of the lower part of the mast, all the way from the boom and up, flattens the sail so that it adapts itself to squalls, and the boat moves along at speed instead of heeling over. P21

Bend the lower part of the mast
1 in light airs and across smooth water, in order to flatten the lower two-thirds of your mainsail
2 when the luff of the sail is backwinded
3 when the sail has too much fullness
4 in strong winds in smooth water.

F50

X }

The Dragon *Debutant*, sailed by the Sundelin brothers of Sweden, 1968 Olympic 5.5-metre champions

46

Straighten the lower part of the mast
1 when sailing in heavy swell and waves,
in order to give the sail greater fullness
and the boat more drive through the
water.

Bend your mast laterally to leeward
1 in strong winds when the sail is too
full in the head
2 in strong winds when the whole sail
has too much fullness.

Bend your mast laterally to windward
1 in order to give the sail greater fullness
and to point high.

A mast which is straight in the lateral
plane enables the boat to point high into
the wind; one that bends will not enable
to boat to point so high.

A bendy boom was thought to be a great help when sailing to windward in weak and strong winds. A sail with too much fullness in the foot could be flattened by bending the boom with a hard pull of the mainsheet. At the same time, however, the luff of the jib would be slackened, the mast would bend less and flatten the luff of the sail less, and the leech would tend to close in the upper part of the sail. For this reason, in a strong wind we must use a rigid boom in order to achieve good pointing and speed.

Boom A, which is flexible at the clew, gives in a squall, reducing the resistance of the sail to the wind and at the same time slacking the leech. F51

A mainsail should be sheeted in such a way that the leech does not point to windward of the course steered. F52

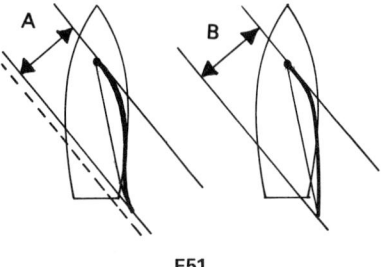

F51

Set your mainsheet further to leeward
1 when the sail has a lot of fullness
2 when the jib does not overlap the main
3 in strong breezes on a flat sea.

Set your mainsheet further inboard
1 to increase the slot between the genoa and the mainsail
2 when the sail is flat
3 in big waves with slack sheets, in order to give twist to the upper part of the sail yet retaining plenty of fullness.

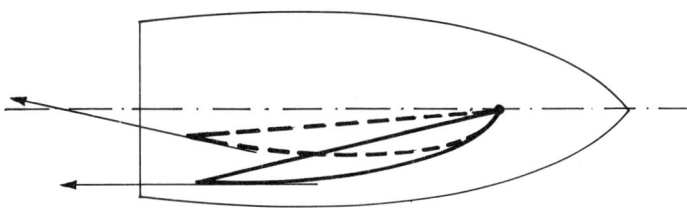

F52

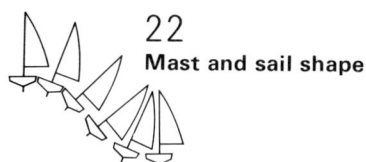

P22

P23

Photos 23–26: Michael Richardson

The curve in the lower portion of the mast gives flexibility to the leech, which allows the air stream to run off it more easily, a decisive factor in light airs. Note the piece of elastic which is only used while training, as it spoils the air flow over the main to some extent. P22

These OK dinghies have leeches which are too tight, causing them to heel excessively. As they are close together and nearing a mark, the crews are leaning forward to see under the sails, thus increasing the angle of heel. By leaning out, they would counteract heeling rather than contributing to it, and would still be able to see under the sails, which would be easier with the boats more upright. P23

The winning boat in the 1967 OK National Championships, sailed by Michael Rich-

P24

P25

ardson, shown going to windward and downwind with the same mast and sail. This particular mast had comparatively little sideways bend, but was more flexible higher up. The resulting sail twist was very effective in strong breezes when going to windward, but less so downwind because of the 'airplane prop' effect. The rig—mast and sail—was a specialised heavy weather rig, and illustrates the point that there is no single optimum shape for all courses or all wind conditions. Note the upright sailing position. Natural weight of $10\frac{1}{2}$ stone can be as high as 14 stone with wet sweaters. P24, P25

Georg Bruder sailing with a Bruder mast. The kicking strap has been set up to maintain leech tension at the expense of flattening the sail slightly. It is the leech which provides the greatest power in downwind sailing and it must not be too free, especially with a straight mast, or power is lost. P26

Weight
By heeling and moving weight forward
the lee bow is immersed, which gives an
asymmetrical hull shape, increases lateral
resistance and decreases wetted surface.
The wedge-shaped section encourages
the bow of the boat to lift to windward,
improving pointing in light airs. Keeping
weight towards the centre of the boat
reduces the pitching moment and thus
maintains the air flow over the sails at a
more constant direction and velocity;
this effect occurs in both rough and
smooth conditions. P27

Use as little helm as possible when going
about. Move over to the other side and
let the boat steer herself round. Correct
your course with the helm when the
sails fill on the new tack.

Running and broad reaching
Make sure the slot between jib and
mainsail is the same width all the way up.
Keep the boom in position with the
kicking strap without tightening the sail.
Increase your speed by moving aft whenever the wind permits, and heel your

51

P28

P29

boat a little to windward in order to get her to steer herself. Sail with as little centreplate as possible in the water.

Tendency to nosedive when reaching and running is overcome on these boats by trapezing off the back beam. The light hull weight causes low inertia and loss of speed if the boat is allowed to dig into waves. This is an example of the necessity to keep weight aft in downwind sailing. The diamond shrouds allow the mast to be over-rotated to fair into the sail, reducing turbulence at the luff. P28, P29

Photos: Michael Richardson

Running
Course
Always steer in such a way that the wind strikes the luff first whenever possible. In many boats it pays to 'tack downwind' rather than sail the straight course to the mark.

A Finn dinghy moves best when the sail is eased out more than 90 degrees to the longitudinal axis in light weather, and the hull heeled slightly to windward. This reduces wetted surface and brings the centre of effort of the single sail over the centreline of the hull, thus reducing the need for corrective helm to maintain a straight course, and reducing rudder drag.

Rigging
Sail with slack rigging and the mast canted forward, but wedge it so that it does not whip from side to side. Increase the sail area by pulling on the kicking strap.

Weight correctly distributed when running before the wind. No backwash from the counter. Weight well forward and low in the centre of the boat

P30

Weight wrongly distributed. Considerable backwash, which reduces speed. The crew is sitting too far aft and too high; the result is that the boat is unsteady

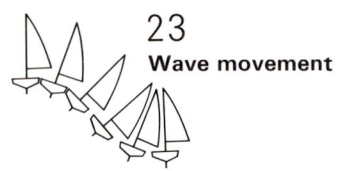

23
Wave movement

A wave fortunately moves up and down in one place, otherwise in a strong wind a boat would be swept away on the surface of the water by the speed of the wave, and broken up on the rocks.

A wave consists of a large number of water particles in motion, and the wave itself rotates. A small wave moves across the surface of the water at a greater speed than a large wave, and it contributes to building up the large waves. F53

Waves are long and flat in deep water, and offer very pleasant sailing conditions. Water and air currents behave in the same way. In the trough of a wave the current and the wind are both turbulent.

In shallow waters near a coast, and in sounds and estuaries, waves change their shape. They become steeper with less distance between crests, and sailing conditions become more difficult. You can parry the crest of a wave by sailing parallel to it before it reaches you, and then sailing over it. F55

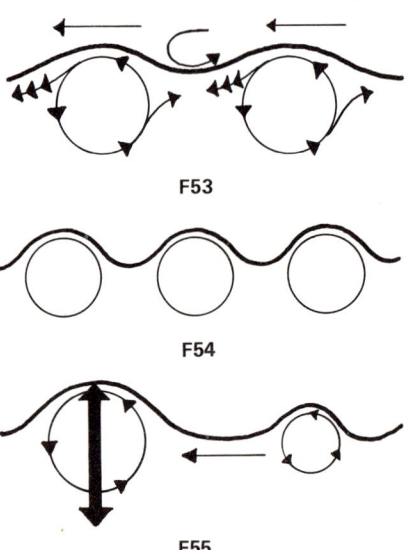

F53

F54

F55

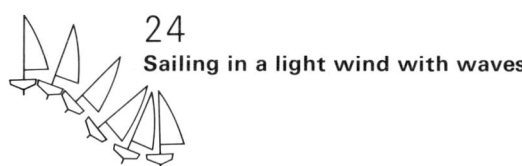

Sailing in a light wind with waves

Beating

Keep your boat running at speed and avoid the steeper waves by sailing parallel to them. Use sails with plenty of fullness in order to regain your momentum after a wave has reduced your speed. The rigging should be slack, but not slack enough to allow the mast to sway as the boat moves through the waves.

Three of the world's best helmsmen training together a few days before the Olympics at Acapulco. From left: Peder Lunde (Norway), John Albrechtson (Sweden) and Paul Elvstrøm (Denmark). The result of this training trip was the completely tuned mast with which Peder Lunde won his silver medal. The shadow on the sail of N 5303 shows that the topmost part of the sail is correctly set to the wind, unlike the sails on the Swedish and Danish boats, which have excessive bend at the mast tops. P32

Course: don't pinch, and don't sail straight into a wave. Sail in such a way that the boat has as little wave resistance as possible.

P32

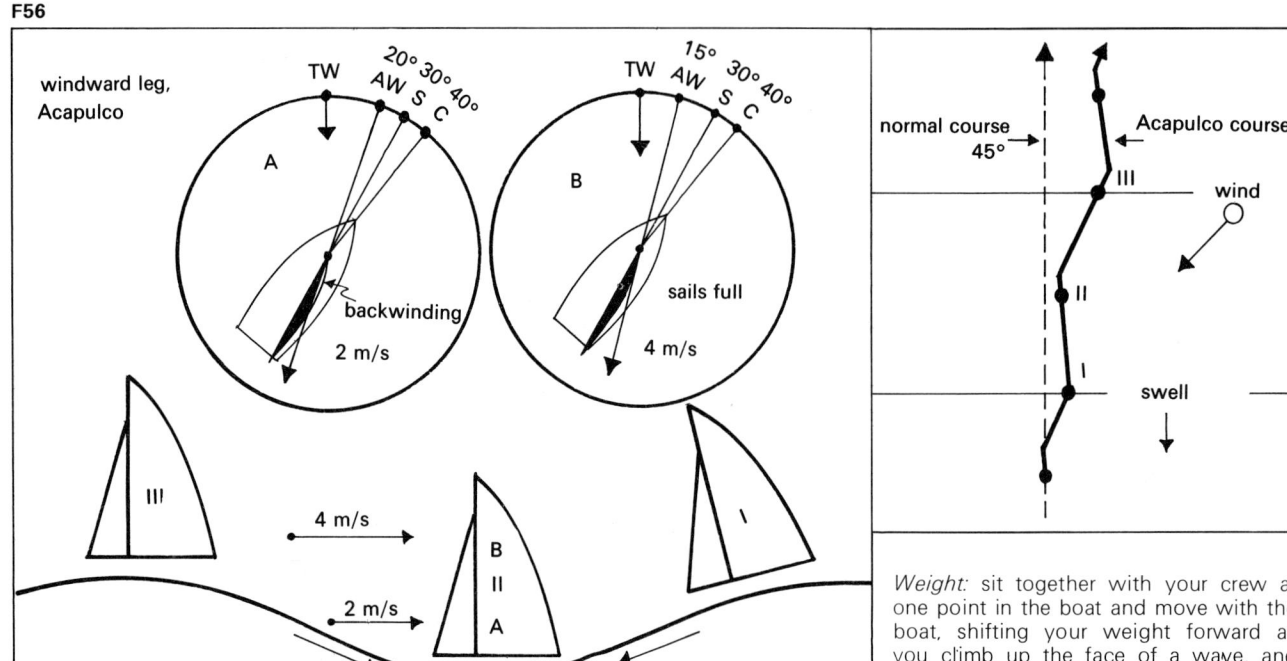

F56

windward leg, Acapulco

A
TW
20° 30° 40°
AW S C
backwinding
2 m/s

B
TW
15° 30° 40°
AW S C
sails full
4 m/s

III
4 m/s
B II A
2 m/s
I

normal course 45°
Acapulco course
III
wind
II
I
swell

Weight: sit together with your crew at one point in the boat and move with the boat, shifting your weight forward as you climb up the face of a wave, and aft as the boat descends into the trough.

Willi Kühweide, shifting forward to get out of a trough
Photo: Michael Richardson

Heel the boat a fraction, and swing your body in and out to ensure that the angle of the sails to the surface of the water is constant. Allow your boat to sail her own course in a big swell. P32

Don't try to change the rhythm of the boat by constantly shifting your weight to change the angle of heel. You will merely succeed in increasing the wave resistance and reducing the speed of your boat.

Sailing in a swell (F56)
Boat I is sliding down into a trough, and the force of gravity is exerted on the leech. In a case like this, a mast that is curved aft is best. Boat II is at the bottom of the trough and is exposed to two wind currents striking the sail at A and B with a speed of 2 and 4 metres per second respectively. The circles are compass cards showing what happens to the wind indicator or apparent wind AW, the true wind TW, the sail S and the course C. Circle B shows the upper part of the sail, which is exposed to a constant wind strength of 4 metres per second. The apparent wind is 15 degrees off the true wind, and the sails are filled the whole time. Circle A shows the apparent wind on the lower portion of the sail. It has moved 5 degrees closer to the course steered by the boat.

Boat II: the helmsman realises that his main is being backwinded. The reason is that the boat has gathered momentum down the face of the wave, while the true wind is weaker in the trough and the apparent wind is blowing at a more acute angle owing to the speed of the boat. In this situation a sail with a flatter lower portion will give the best results.

Boat III: as the boat slows down, the apparent wind draws free once again and the helmsman can sail closer to the wind as he moves up the crest of the wave. On the crest the boat again meets a wind of 4 metres per second, and the result is that the lower portion of the mainsail is backwinded by the jib, if course is not altered.

Bottom left: a sensible way of sailing to windward in a swell and a light breeze, corresponding to the situation shown in the upper diagram.

Broad reaching
Don't get into a situation where your boat is stuck in a trough, and you are trying

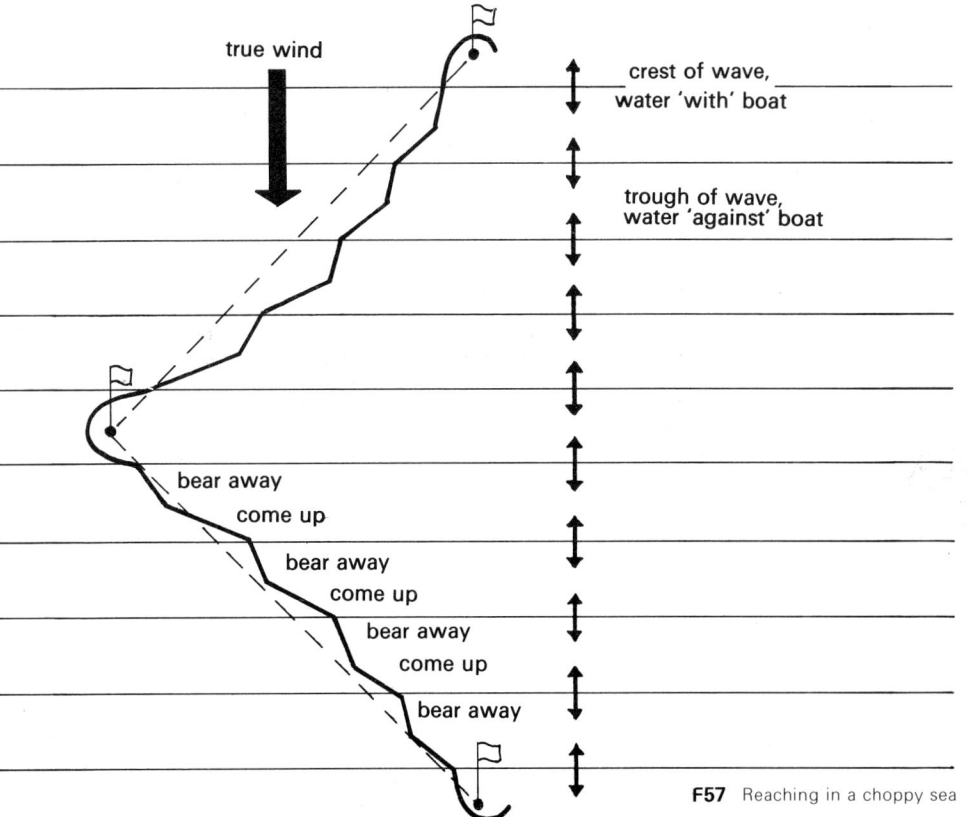

true wind

crest of wave, water 'with' boat

trough of wave, water 'against' boat

bear away

come up

bear away

come up

bear away

come up

bear away

F57 Reaching in a choppy sea

to get out of it by sitting well back in the stern. P33

When your boat has lost speed and is lifting her bows, the reason is that a wave has overtaken her and is running under the hull. In this situation the helmsman should move his weight forward, come up into the wind and haul in on the sheet in order to get up enough speed to take up a position ahead of the next wave that is coming along, utilising its speed to get his boat planing again.

A good helmsman can make a downwind leg look like one long surf ride by catching waves correctly. It is possible to retain speed on a broad reach by bearing away with the waves and luffing in the troughs, sailing a zig-zag course in order to take full advantage of wave movement. F57

Running
Pull in on the kicking strap, taking care not to spoil the shape of the sail, and curve the mast in order to increase the sail area. (F58) The apparent wind is

very weak in light airs, and when the boat sails down the face of a wave the apparent wind is practically nil. For this reason you should steer on a zig-zag course with repeated gybes in order to get the wind in the sails. This is more important still when the current is with you. Give your mast a forward rake if possible, and keep a careful eye on the waves. Pick out a small wave—it will be moving faster—and sail across to it, staying with it as long as possible. Work the helm and trim the sails so that the speed of your boat is equal to that of the wave. Don't leave it until just before it has developed into a large wave: this is the time to leave it, or you will find yourself stuck in a trough.

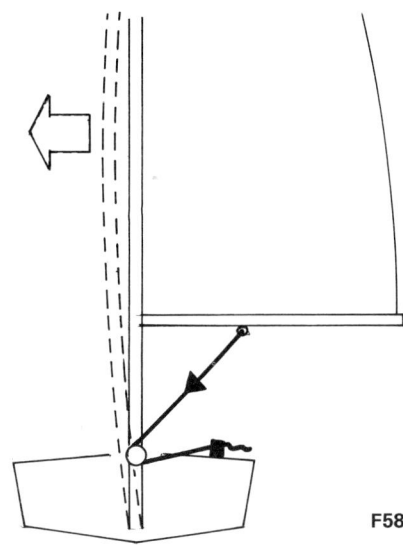

F58

To windward

A light, modern sailing boat can develop an apparent wind of over 15 metres per second when sailing to windward. To achieve this, the wind must strike and leave the sail without being obstructed. Trim your sail so that the luff and the leech do not stall in a strong wind.

A good basis of comparison is to be found in the exhaust of a car engine and the leading edge of an aeroplane wing. Racing motorists often polish the insides of exhausts in order to give the exhaust gases an unimpeded outlet, thereby giving the engine a greater power. Similarly, a pilot takes great care to check the leading edge of his wing. It must be quite smooth, in order to give the surface of the wing maximum lift. If the leading edge is rough, as can happen with icing, the aerodynamic force is upset, and the aircraft is liable to crash.

The forward section of the sail is most important, because the camber in this part of the sail produces an aerodynamic force which works in a more forward direction than the aerodynamic forces in other parts of the sail.

In order to prevent this camber from being pressed out of shape by squalls of wind, the shape of the sail must be adjusted to the increased wind force in the squalls *before* these strike the sail. If this is not done in time, the boat will heel over instead of accelerating in a strong wind. F35

The leech should be pulled straight down to the sheeting point in a strong wind, to prevent it flapping. The harder it blows, the further to leeward your sail should be sheeted, in order to prevent the boat heeling over.

Modern sheeting technique involves using the sheet horse instead of regulating the sheet. Cords are fastened to the sheet block, which slides across the horse. The helmsman pulls the sail down to leeward or up to windward with the line, as the wind increases or decreases in strength. Flow can be shifted forward by increasing luff tension with the Cun-

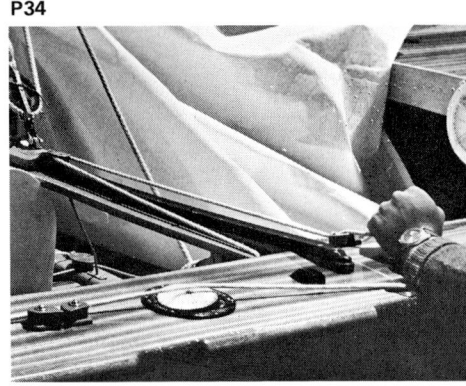

Sheet horse tackle on the FD *Tine*

Peter White and John Davies in their 505 demonstrate how these boats should be handled in a breeze. The boom has been sheeted down to leeward and the boat is sailing upright and completely balanced. Luff tension has been increased by using the Cunningham hole
Photo: Michael Richardson

Expert Danish heavy weather Finn sailor Henning Wind, Finn Gold Cup, Whitstable, 1969
Photo: Michael Richardson

ningham hole, or aft by decreasing tension. P34, F36, F37

In a squall helmsman and crew should keep close together, so that the boat can move freely round one centre of gravity.

Course

Sailing in squally weather is most exciting, and very difficult to master perfectly. To do this, one must know how the wind blows in a squall. Usually squalls come in pairs: first a small one and then shortly afterwards a more powerful one. The small squall is heralded by the characteristic flapping of the sail which makes it so awkward to discover the actual direction of the wind.

Don't bother about the way the wind is behaving: just continue straight ahead on your tack. A little later the more powerful squall will come, and this is the one to try to utilise. Do not go about after the little squall has passed.

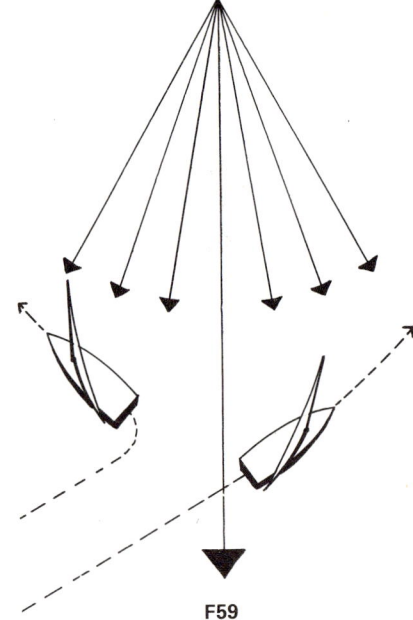

F59

Wind in a squall

Look at the water to windward, pick out a big squall, sheet the boom hard down to leeward, trim your sheets and steer a little higher into the wind, so that the sails can meet the squall at a more acute angle when it comes.

Luff through the squall and steer so that the sails cut through the puffs of wind at a sharper angle than usual, in order to prevent the boat heeling. As your boat emerges from the squall it will encounter weaker wind strengths and the apparent wind will move forward, since the boat's apparent wind is greater than the true wind. Sail straight on, if necessary easing off a little in order to maintain speed. After a short while the wind strength will stabilise: it will blow more evenly and once again you can sail a normal wind-ward tack. In order to practise this squall technique for flat water, which generally puts a less observant rival many yards astern and to leeward, the sails must be hauled in quite flat and sheeted down all the way to leeward. If the sails flap in the wind you will not be able to get enough speed or point as high.

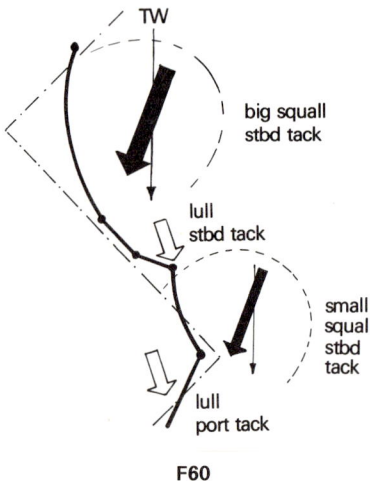

TW

big squall stbd tack

lull stbd tack

small squall stbd tack

lull port tack

F60

Sailing in squalls

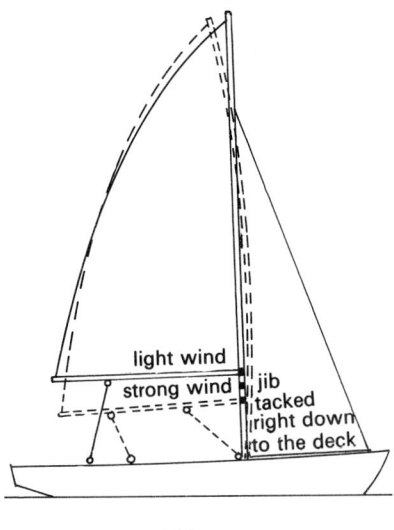

light wind

strong wind | jib tacked right down to the deck

F61

Cleat your sheets and go out and learn this technique. You will probably capsize a number of times before you have mastered it, and it may take you some time. But once you have learnt it, not many helmsmen will leave you behind in conditions of this kind.

Set of sails on mast and jibstay
For squalls the boom should be on the lower mark to ensure that the boat can stand more wind. Tighten the downhaul and sheet, and bend the mast in order to flatten the sail. In light airs and breezes, set the boom at the highest mark. In both cases the jib should be tacked right down at deck level in order to close the slot between the deck and the sail. F61, F49

Broad reaching
Ease off on the sheet, bear away in the squalls, and keep the boat upright. In order to increase speed the sail should be sheeted out so far that the aerodynamic force coincides with the course steered. F62

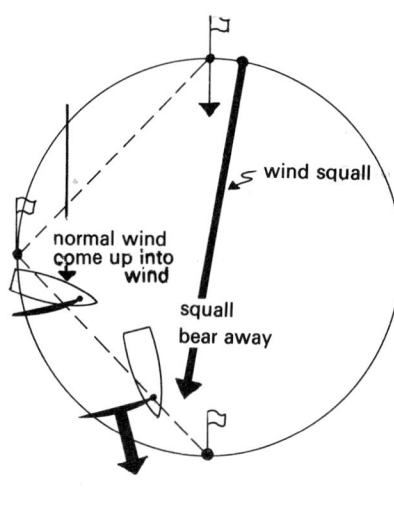

wind squall

normal wind come up into wind

squall bear away

F62

P37
Bjørn Lofterød, at the age of 12, making good speed on the reach, and with his weight correctly positioned

Tighten the leech with the downhaul in order to do this, otherwise the sail will flap in the wind. Keep your weight aft. P38

Running
Bear away before squalls and luff up between them. Practise the reaching technique as far as possible. Use the more powerful squalls as a pointer for the course you are steering. Sail with the squalls in the direction in which they are blowing, so that the boat remains planing as long as possible. The aim is for the boat to plane at full speed. It does not matter whether your boat is pointing to windward or leeward of the mark, even if this means lengthening the course.

P38
Perfect balance on a broad reach, with the whole mainsail pulling effectively. The downhaul has been properly tightened so as to keep the boom down. The Knudsen brothers in a Trapeze

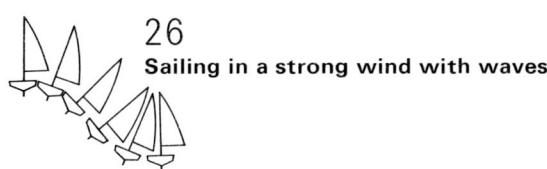

26

Sailing in a strong wind with waves

Beating
Do not sail your boat straight through big waves. If you do this, it will not pick up speed until it is too late. A boat sailing at reduced speed has a much smaller chance of regaining its speed when sailing against waves.

With plenty of fullness in your sail you will be able to pick up speed more quickly, after the boat has been stopped by a wave.

F63

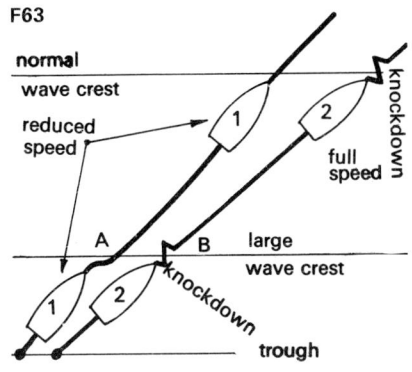

normal
wave crest
reduced speed
knockdown
1   2
full speed
A   B   large
wave crest
knockdown
1   2
trough

The boat must not be allowed to choose its own way through the waves. It must be steered the whole time to keep the sails at the most advantageous angle in relation to the apparent wind, which will be moving forward when the boat is sailing at speed down the windward side of the wave, and veering abeam when the boat sails more slowly up the lee side of the wave. Observe your wind indicator.

Keep a constant eye on the waves. If there is smoother water to windward or leeward make your way there, so that you encounter reduced wave resistance. There will be a succession of waves: luff up and reduce speed in front of the first one. Sail straight through it if possible, or sail over it, bearing away slightly. You may have gained a fraction to windward and you will have got just as far as the boat sailing straight ahead at full speed and then being stopped by a wave. Continue up the next wave with the same favourable windward course and reduce speed, thus gaining a valuable lead over your rival. You will finally end up well to windward of your opponent,

who will have vainly tried to fight through the wave crests at too great a speed.

In a steep seaway and with continuous wave resistance the same advantage can be achieved by pinching to windward. The waves present so much resistance that the boat will not attain full speed, even if every effort is made to do so. The winner will be the helmsman who manages to sail his boat as high into the wind and at as great a speed as conditions allow. F63

Go about when the waves allow. Do not attempt to do so if there is a risk that a wave might stop the boat before full speed has been reached on the fresh tack. Use as little helm as possible and allow the boat to decide its own rhythm as you go about. Do not ease off your jib until the very last moment. Maintain the speed and rhythm of the boat, and bring it smartly around as you move from leeward to windward. Trim your sheets very carefully on the new tack and do not pull in on your sheets until the boat is moving at full speed.

P39

A too-rigid mast will give a full mainsail the wrong shape in a squall. As a result the boat will not accelerate

Reaching and running

Make full use of squalls and bear away as you pass through them. Sail on a zig-zag course, utilising the waves.

There is great risk of capsizing when gybing in heavy seas. Most helmsmen believe the best moment to gybe is when the boat is moving at reduced speed. They soon discover their mistake! The reason is that when speed is reduced the pressure of the wind on the sails is greatest, and the boat will capsize as the main comes across.

The safest moment to gybe is when the boat is planing at full speed. The wind pressure will then be least. Pull in on the sheet, bear away and bring the boom smartly across as you move across the boat. At the same time use your helm to luff up slightly into the wind on your new tack, and everything will be under control.

If you're caught out

1 get a good grip on the bow and turn it so that the boat is pointing into the

Tom Skjønberg in the Kiel Regatta, 1968

P41 **P40**

P42

67

P43

F64

wind

B   A

water resistance

wind. Get hold of the sheet and ease it right out

2 scramble on board, take the helm, and bear away

3 bear away until you are broad reaching and then running. Get speed up and set about unshipping the water. A dinghy should have two automatic self-drainers which operate as soon as they are opened by the helmsman. P40–43

Raise the centreplate in very strong squalls. A is drifting to leeward, and heeling over less. B encounters greater water resistance, and risks capsizing. F64

Use your spinnaker like a genoa, setting it so as to achieve the greatest possible area by raising the spinnaker boom so that the leeches have a good spread. Only a few spinnakers are efficient when the boom is resting on the forestay. The aerodynamic force of the sail must be moved further forward in order to pull in the same direction as the boat is sailing. In order to achieve this the spinnaker boom should be moved 8–10 in. to windward of the forestay when broad reaching. When we raise the boom on a reach the sail spreads and flattens, and we can sail higher. The sail will be pulling most effectively when we ease off the sheet so that the windward leech is just about to collapse. P44, F65

This 505 spinnaker is set for maximum effect. The two clews are at the same height above the water, and the shape of the sail is symmetrical. The sheet is eased to the point where the windward luff is just on the point of collapse. The foot of the sail opens out on a reach, allowing air flow downwards and reducing the heeling moment. (A cupped foot

tends to direct the flow upwards). Larger spreaders might control the topmast better, but would reduce performance to windward. The amount of sideways bend above the spreaders is not excessive and is typical for a pear-shaped mast with the boom let out, as the stress is on the weakest dimension of the mast. P44

The bow launcher system of spinnaker setting
This system for spinnaker launching and recovery was pioneered by Roger Green of Canada, and developed by the top FD crews in 1968. The halyard is led aft from the mast to the helmsman and returns through a tube about 5 in. in

F65

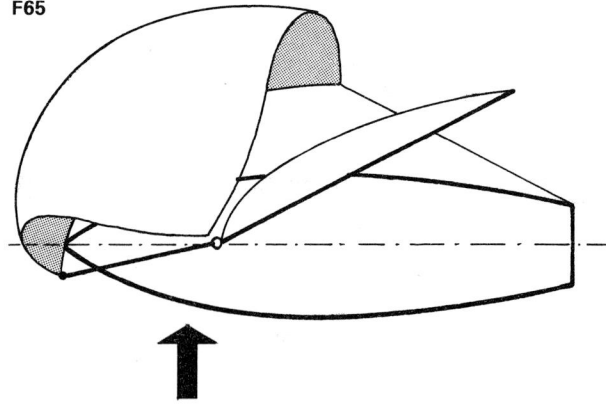

diameter below the foredeck where it emerges forward of the forestay through a polished 'trumpet' mouth and is attached to the spinnaker just below centre. Thus the helmsman can release the halyard and retract the spinnaker with the downhaul line. The spinnaker turns inside out and disappears into the chute, leaving only the head and clews at the mouth ready for the next hoist. It is possible by this means to hoist and lower the spinnaker while the crew remains on the trapeze on a close reach if a luffing match develops or the wind changes direction.

Photo: Michael Richardson

Modern Finn and OK masts

The flexible mast has an advantage in light airs when going to windward, in that the helmsman need not use the mainsheet to adjust sail shape, and in strong winds by freeing the leech and reducing the heeling moment. But when reaching and running, and when beating in medium wind conditions, the stiff mast has definite advantages.

A stiff mast has an even curve which follows the luff of the sail. In the lateral plane it is rigid until about a metre from the top, where it tapers almost to a point. This taper is even more important in a Finn than an OK due to the narrower head of the sail, and the greater weight of the boat relative to that of the helms-man.

When broad reaching and running, a boat with a rigid mast accelerates more quickly. The sail catches the wind, and the wind escapes from the sail with less resistance because the top of the mast bends forward.

See Chapter 22 on mast and sail shape.

I am convinced that any helmsman who hopes to win high honours in international sailing must first of all have a thorough practical knowledge of dinghy sailing.

Practice in sailing with a flexible rig and with the movable weight correctly placed are the two most important skills required of a crew to achieve maximum speed in a modern light keelboat. Dinghy sailors have learnt this, and they have a great advantage over the helmsman who learns his sailing in a keelboat.

Three persons on board a 5.5-metre represent a weight of a quarter of a ton. If they are wrongly placed, the boat's rhythm is destroyed. In a Soling the crew weigh one-quarter of the total weight of the boat, and the importance of correct weight placement is greater still.

P45

P46

Note how gracefully and easily a 5.5-metre behaves at sea. *Fram IV* lifts her bows with the same ease as a dinghy without the crew having to move. The reverse transom absorbs the stern wave, as well as giving the boat a longer waterline

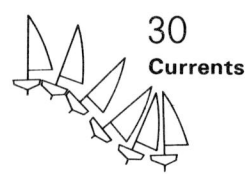

The current we sail in may be composed
of three different currents:
1 the meteorological current, which runs
in one particular direction, independent
of local coastal currents
2 tidal currents, which change direction
and strength in relation to the times of
high and low tide
3 wind-motivated currents, which are
surface currents driven by the wind.
Their direction is 30–45 degrees to the
right (clockwise) of the true wind. They
have a force of about $\frac{1}{4}$ knot in a wind
of 10 knots.

In other words, a current affecting sailing
could be:
1 a wind-driven current, when there is a
wind blowing on waters otherwise free
from currents
2 a meteorological or tidal current, when
there is no wind
3 a mixture of the above.

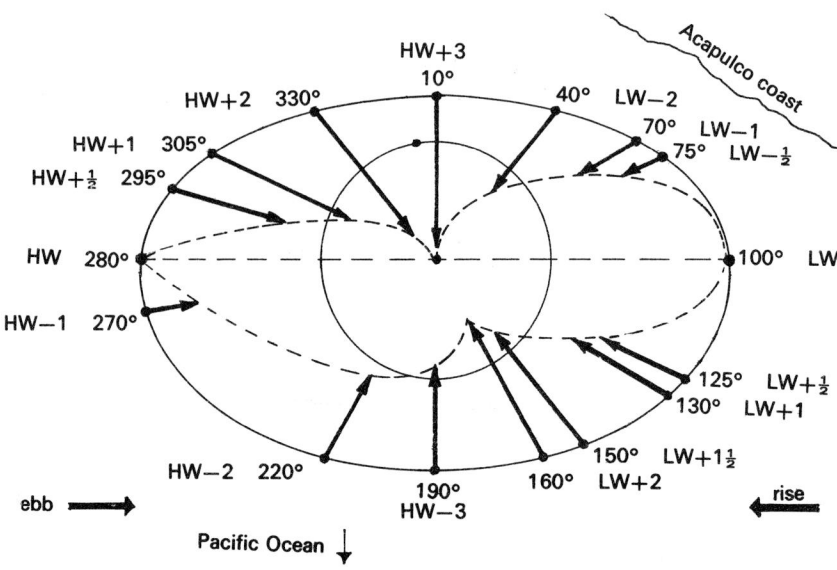

F66

Direction and speed of current in the sea off a
straight coastline. Observations made by the
author at Acapulco, 1968

F66 shows the current off Acapulco, where there is a shoreline running from 110 to 290 degrees, with open sea outside. High tide (left) 280 degrees, and low tide (right) 100 degrees. The lengths of the arrows represent the strength of the current, and their direction the way the current is running. $H+\frac{1}{2}$ hour indicates that the observation of the current has been taken half an hour after high water, $L-1$ hour indicates that it was taken one hour before low water, and so on. In order to arrive at, and use, this calculation one needs a tide table showing times of high water and low water over the course of a day.

The tide level off a coast can be compared to a large wave starting at high water and moving along the coast. It turns at low water and moves back in the opposite direction. The actual tidal stream flows in various directions which rotate with the sun between the hours for high and low water. The current rotates evenly and regularly when it comes from the open sea, but as it is about to turn away from the coast it

meets resistance and may suddenly change from the direction of high tide to low tide (flow and ebb) in the course of an hour. It would, for example, be possible to start at 1 pm, which corresponds to low water—2 hours, with a current moving from 40 degrees and arrive at the finishing line three hours later, at 4 pm, with a current running from 130 degrees.

For this reason it is very important to work out a table showing the variation in the current in the waters you are going to sail in. A change of current is just as important as a change of wind!

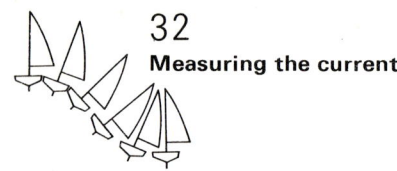

1 Mark north-south lines, making the necessary correction for magnetic variation in the waters around the course. F67

2 Take bearings from the current gauge of three different points marked on the chart, and note the compass bearings and time. F67, F68

3 While the current gauge drifts for half an hour, draw the three bearings on the chart with a protractor, making the necessary allowance for magnetic variation. The point of intersection gives the position (I) of the current gauge. F67, F68

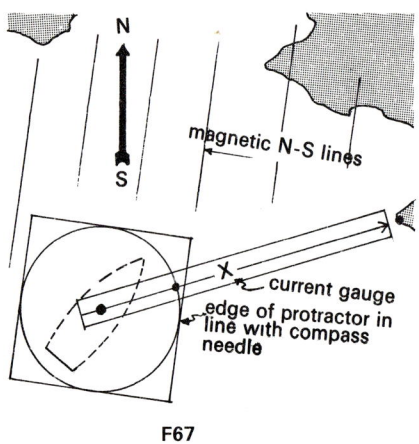

F67

Protractor for taking bearings for plotting current

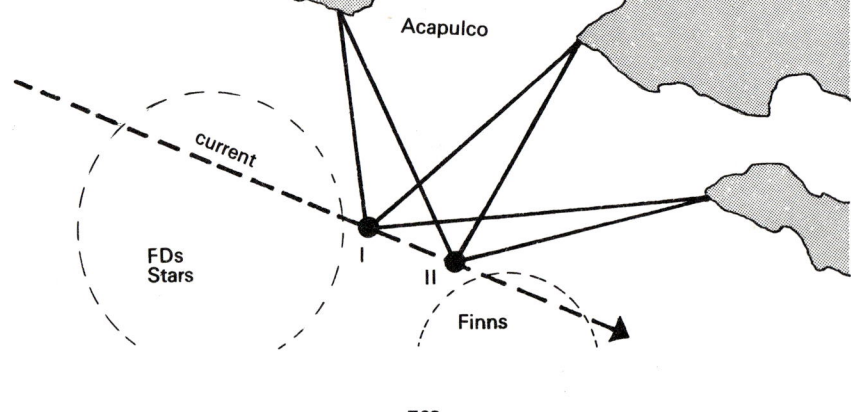

F68

4 After half an hour has elapsed take three new bearings and plot the second position of the current gauge on the chart.

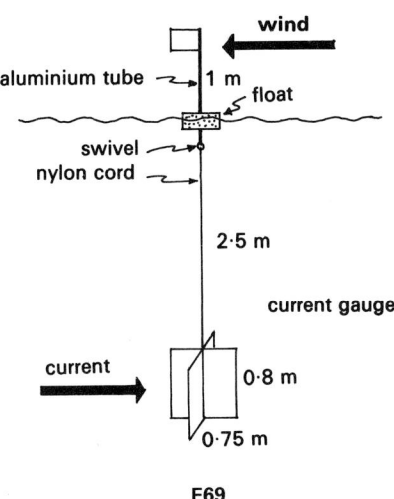

wind

aluminium tube → 1 m

float

swivel →

nylon cord →

2·5 m

current gauge

current →

0·8 m

0·75 m

F69

5 Join position I and position II. Place the protractor parallel with the magnetic north-south lines with its centre over position I, and read off the direction of the line between I and II. This will give you the direction and area from which the current is coming.

6 One can find the speed of the current by comparing the distance between positions I and II with the scale of latitude printed on the edge of the chart. One nautical mile = one minute of latitude.

You should make twelve observations, one for every hour of the tidal period, before drawing a current chart. It is possible to complete the job in a few days or less.

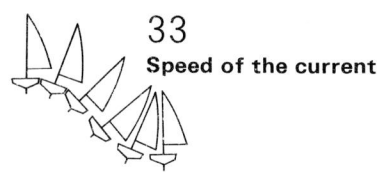
A current runs faster in deep water and more slowly over shallows. It is strongest in the middle of a sound or inlet, and weakest around, in front of and behind islands and along the shore. It runs more strongly where there is land to the right of it. Quite close to the shore a back eddy is produced, which a skilful helmsman can sometimes make good use of. F70

In a following current sail over deep water and in the middle of a sound. In an unfavourable current sail over shallow water, close to land, and over shallows.

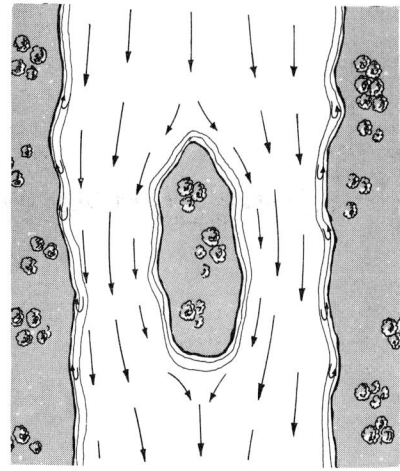

F70

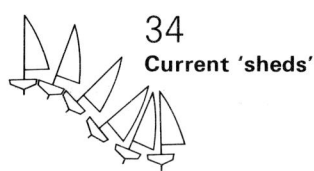

There are three types of current sheds:
Between a less turbulent current running
parallel to a stronger one. In Acapulco,
for example, a shed or dividing line of
this kind occurred fairly frequently. The
water in the less turbulent current had a
brownish colour, while the stronger
currents were pale blue. Between them
the surface was white with foam.

Where one current strikes another at an
oblique angle. This type can also be
recognised by the foam on the surface
of the water. Sheds also may occur where
water from a river meets an ocean-going
current.

Between currents from opposing directions.

Measuring current sheds:
1 Drop a small piece of paper or a
floating object in both currents at the
same time and take a compass bearing
between them.
2 Plot the bearing through positions 1–1.
3 Take a new bearing a few minutes
later and plot the bearing through positions 2–2. Compare the two bearings.
F71

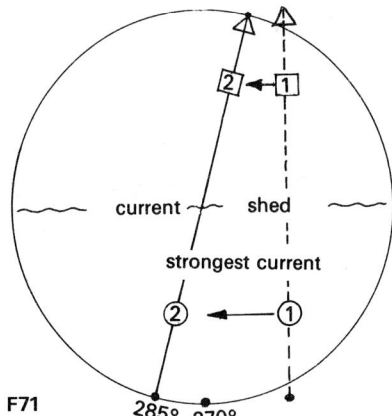

F71

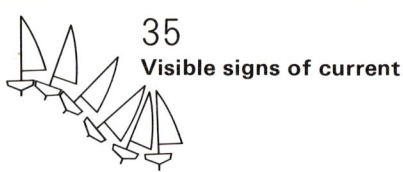

35
Visible signs of current

As a rule we are compelled to judge a current without the help of technical aids.

Current running against a steady wind: steep waves = stronger current; longer and flatter waves = weaker current. Current in the same direction as a steady wind: steep waves = a weaker current; longer, flatter waves = stronger current. When the current is running with a very strong wind: fluted ripples on the water = strong current.
Calm water = weak current flowing at the same speed as the wind.

Most people believe that a current primarily gives a sailing boat leeway, and they try to reduce this by steering in such a way that the current runs along the keel and not at an angle to it, assuming that a larger surface produces more leeway than a smaller surface. This, however, is not correct.

An object dropped into water drifts at the same speed whether it is large or small, heavy or light. It makes no difference whether it is head-on or angled off the current.

Boats X and Y are drifting at the same speed. F72

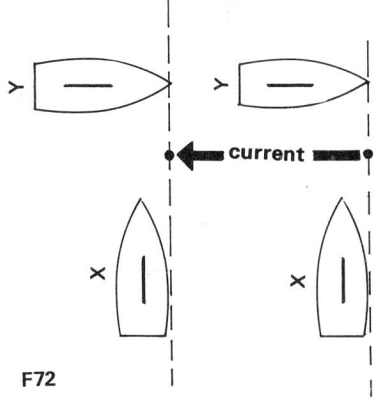

current

F72

Always try to sail to windward with the current on the lee bow. By sailing in this way in a current, we get a stronger apparent wind; when we are sailing to windward with the current abeam, the apparent wind presses the sails out of the true wind and the apparent wind is weaker. F77, F79

If we know the speed of the boat and of the current, we can plot the course of the boat's drift to leeward and the speed over the ground in knots. F73–75

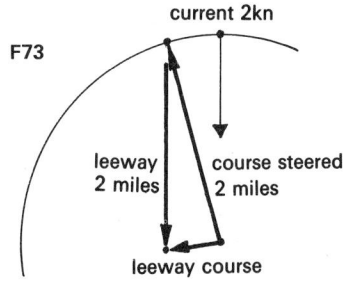

F73

current 2kn

leeway 2 miles

course steered 2 miles

leeway course

sailing against the current

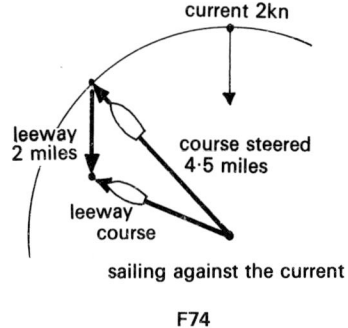

current 2kn

leeway
2 miles

course steered
4·5 miles

leeway
course

sailing against the current

F74

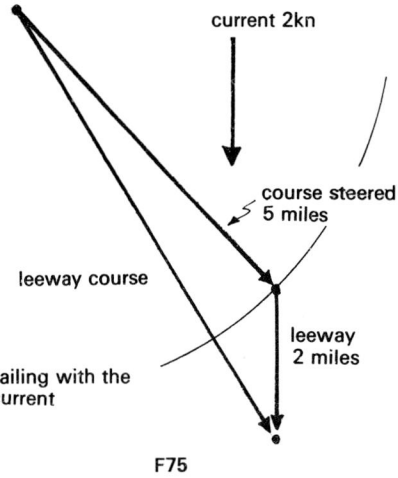

current 2kn

course steered
5 miles

leeway course

leeway
2 miles

sailing with the
current

F75

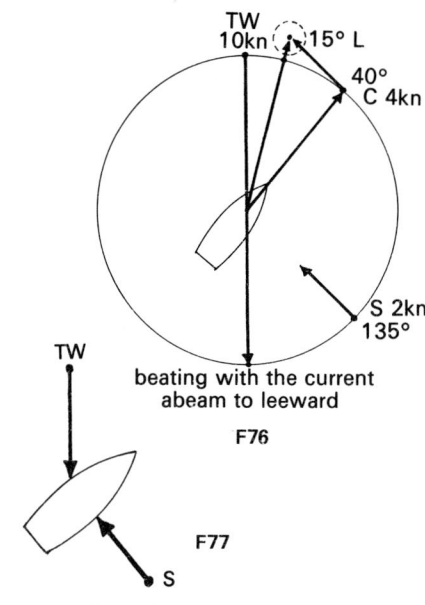

TW
10kn   15° L

40°
C 4kn

S 2kn
135°

TW

beating with the current
abeam to leeward

F76

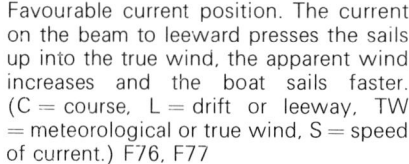

TW

S

current forces boat
against the wind,
increasing pressure

Favourable current position. The current
on the beam to leeward presses the sails
up into the true wind, the apparent wind
increases and the boat sails faster.
(C = course, L = drift or leeway, TW
= meteorological or true wind, S = speed
of current.) F76, F77

F77

Unfavourable current position. The current on the beam to windward pushes the sails away from the true wind. The apparent wind is reduced and the boat sails more slowly. Do not pinch, but bear away on this tack. F78, F79

Sail at full speed on both tacks to achieve maximum speed (AW= apparent or sailing wind). F80

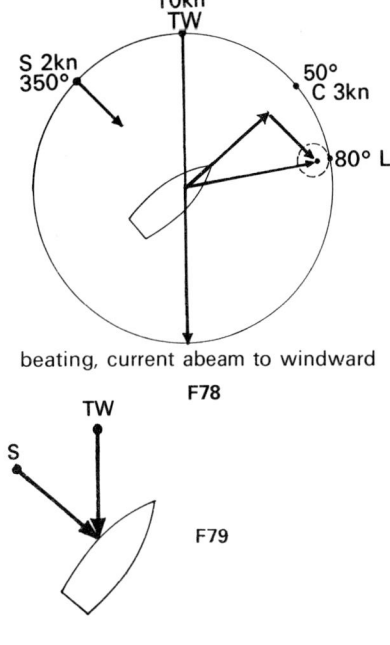

beating, current abeam to windward

F78

current pushes boat off the wind, reducing pressure

F79

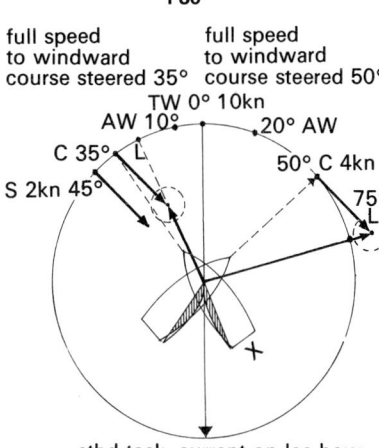

F80

full speed to windward course steered 35°   full speed to windward course steered 50°

stbd tack, current on lee bow
port tack, current abeam to windward

Never pinch in a contrary current. When the wind indicator is in the maximum forward position, the boat is running at full speed. The sails do not show this. They are full, even though we are pinching, because the apparent wind is moving against the true wind when the speed is reduced. F81

Boat X will reach the windward mark first because it has laid a course not so close to the wind but giving greater speed, whereas Y is pinching and will lose. F82

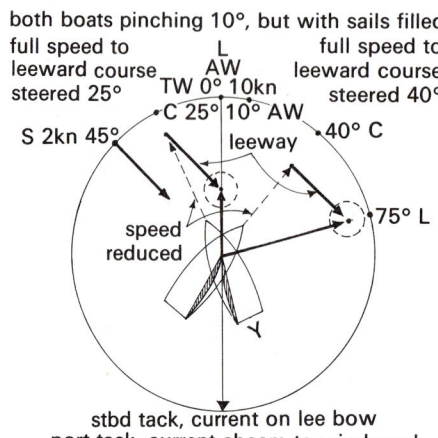

both boats pinching 10°, but with sails filled

full speed to leeward course steered 25°

full speed to leeward course steered 40°

L
AW
TW 0° 10kn
C 25° 10° AW
S 2kn 45°
leeway
40° C
75° L
speed reduced
Y

stbd tack, current on lee bow
port tack, current abeam to windward

F81

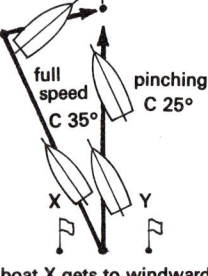

full speed
C 35°

pinching
C 25°

X   Y

boat X gets to windward mark first (F80)
boat Y is outsailed (F81)

F82

Course steered and course made good in a current

The diagram shows a keen struggle to reach the windward mark first. It helps to close the shore and find shallower water, a less choppy sea and less current. F83

Starboard tack gives an unfavourable position in the current. Do not pinch, but fill the sails. Cross the starting line on the port tack to gain the advantage of lee-bowing. It is easy to overstand the mark on the last beat on the port tack and to fail to fetch it on the starboard tack. F84

Cross the starting line on the port tack, so as to lee-bow as quickly as possible to avoid overstanding the mark. Sail on the starboard half of the course. F85

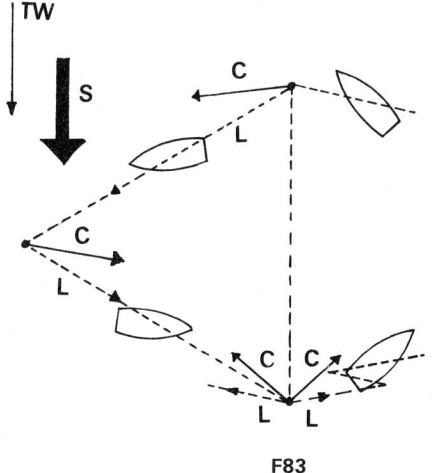

F83

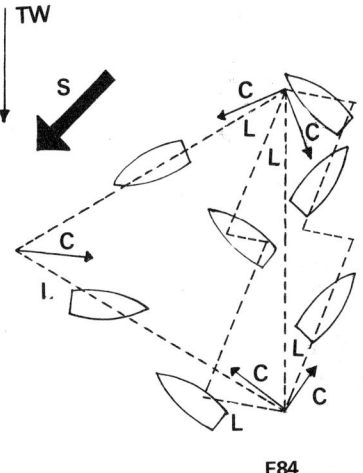

F84

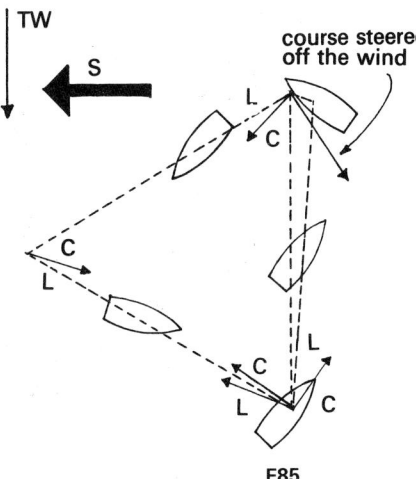

F85

Start on the port tack in order to lee-bow. Sail on the starboard half of the course to avoid overstanding the mark. On the starboard tack, the course steered is almost the same as the direction of drift. F86.

Go about much earlier than you imagine would be correct, in order to make your last tack to the mark. F87

Start on the starboard tack, which will give you a splendid lee-bow situation. Remain on this tack as long as possible, in order not to overstand the mark. F88

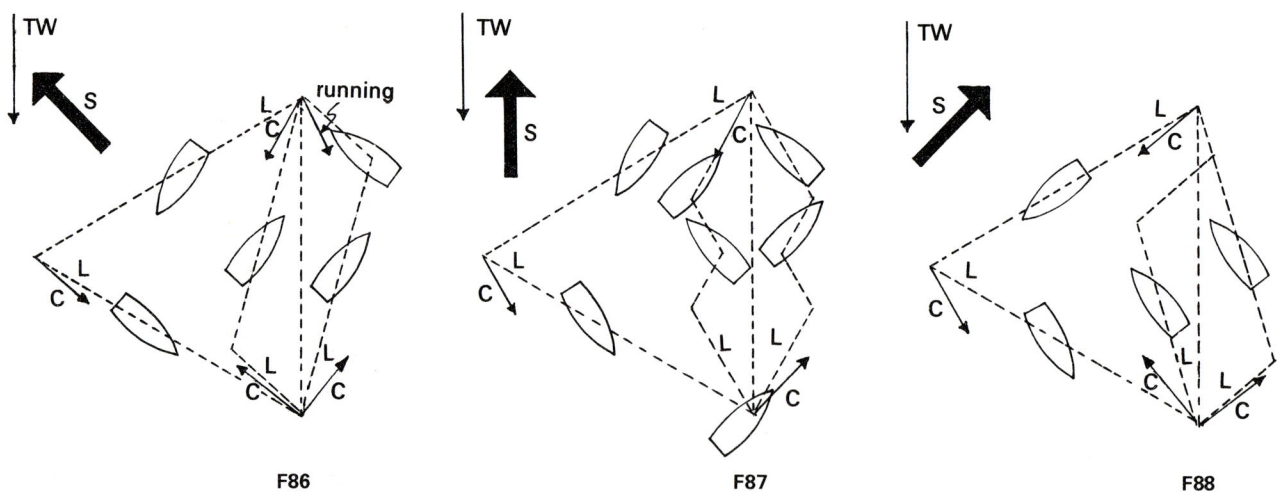

F86

F87

F88

Start on the starboard tack and keep this tack as long as possible. A long beat across to the starboard half of the course would create problems in calculating the last tack on the mark. It is easy to overstand the mark. F89

Sail on the port half of the course and do not go about on the port tack too early. Do not pinch too much on the last tack: the current will drive the boat to windward. F90

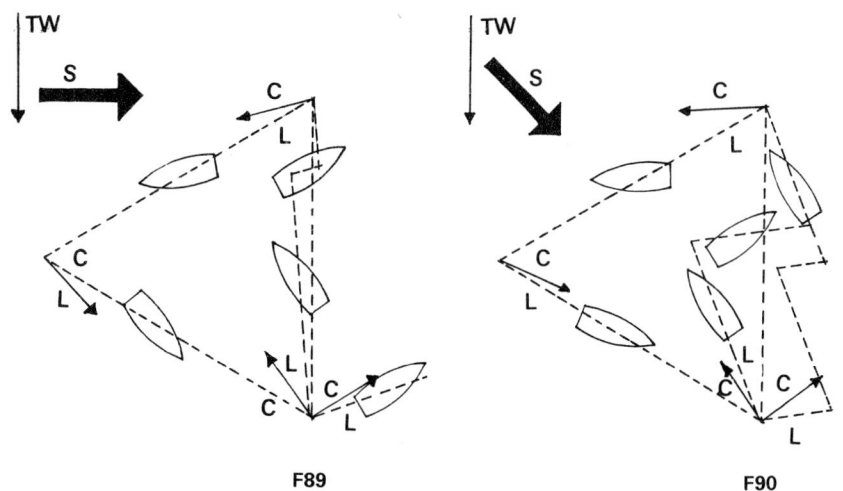

F89

F90

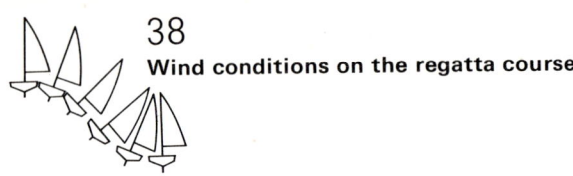

A sailing boat is propelled by the apparent wind. This is the wind on which we must concentrate if we want to sail fast. It is not easy to discover in advance how it will behave during the race, but it is a great help to know what winds it is composed of, and how these behave under various conditions.

Calm weather on the regatta course means that there is an area of high pressure locally, and winds will be light. When the air pressure and the barometer fall it will start to blow from a low pressure area in the vicinity. The low pressure will dislodge the high pressure. There will be a wind blowing between them, anti-clockwise round the low and clockwise round the high. Strong winds are indicated where there are isobar lines running close together on the weather chart (A) and light winds where the isobar lines are spaced further apart (B). F91

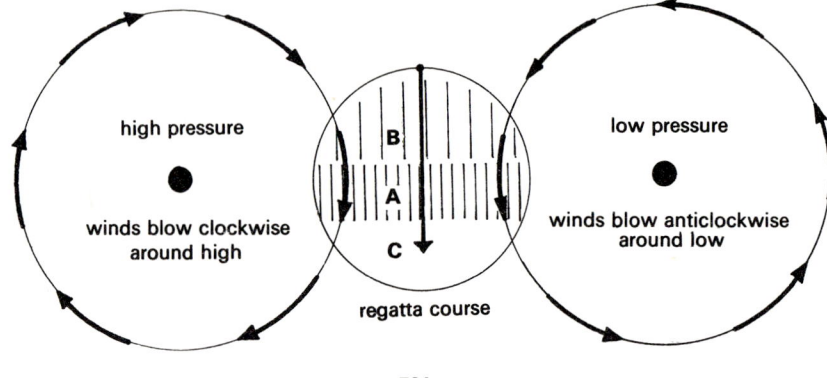

high pressure

winds blow clockwise around high

B
A
C

regatta course

low pressure

winds blow anticlockwise around low

F91

The true wind in which we sail reaches as far as the top of our mast. An isobar wind blowing at an altitude of 1000 metres contains squalls of wind which strike the sails. An isobar wind above 1000 metres may also influence the surface wind. It may be a general powerful current of air gradually turning the lower isobar wind in the same direction. F92

As a general rule, the wind shifts clockwise, the harder it blows.

The difference between a true wind over the sea surface and an isobar wind is 25–30 degrees. A squall from an isobar wind will have lost one-quarter of its wind strength when it strikes the boat. This is owing to friction against the sea, islands etc, as normally its direction is 10–15 degrees to the right of the true wind (as you face it). But a squall of this kind from an isobar wind could very easily come from the left on the day you are racing!

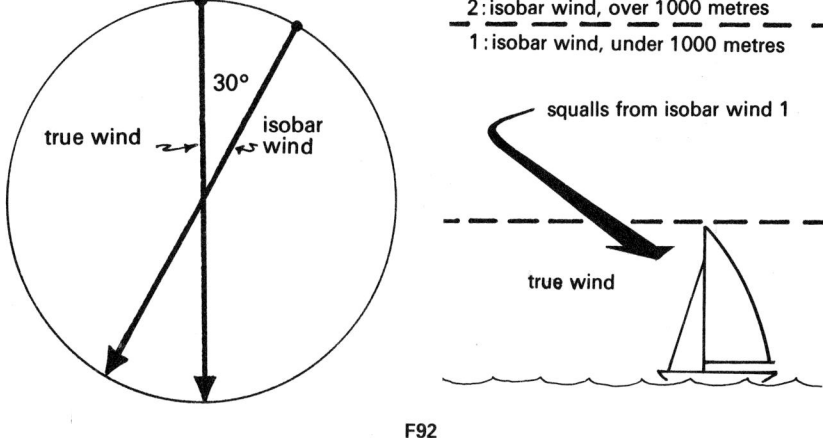

F92

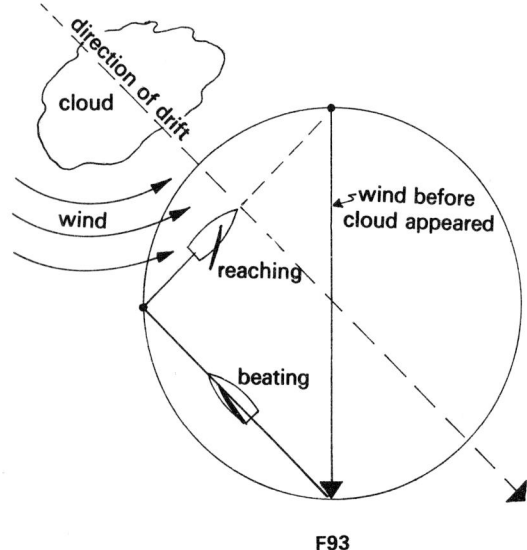

direction of drift

cloud

wind

reaching

wind before cloud appeared

beating

F93

A depression is accompanied by clouds. When these approach, the wind may blow out of the clouds from a little to the left of their general direction of drift. When the cloud passes the wind veers to the right.

This occurred during the final race for Finn dinghies during the World Championships in Hangø, Finland in 1967. Most of the boats quite correctly beat up into the wind in order to meet the cloud, but they held their course too long and were forced to broad reach to the windward mark. F93

Squalls striking on the open sea veer less from the true wind than squalls striking a coastal area. Hilly country produces strong squalls of wind, and for this reason it is really more dangerous to sail in narrow sounds and fjords than on the open sea.

The temperature often occasions considerable wind shifts. When a warm current of air approaches, the isobar wind veers to the right. When colder air approaches, it backs to the left. If the isobar wind blows downward, it may occasion a shift of wind.

39
Wind speed table

Beaufort	Knots	Metres per second (approx.)
0	less than 1	0–0.5
1	1–3	0.5–1.5
2	4–6	2.0–3.1
3	7–10	3.6–5.1
4	11–16	5.7–8.2
5	17–21	8.7–10.8
6	22–27	11.3–13.8
7	28–33	14.4–16.9
8	34–40	17.4–20.5

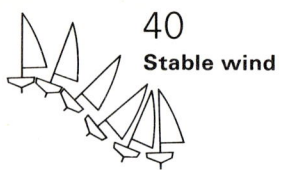

The wind shown is perfectly even, without any variation in direction or strength. It does not blow in an upward direction and it is not reinforced by any squalls from the isobar wind. The wind strength is constant and it feels stronger than it is. It blows more horizontally, and makes sailing to windward wearisome. Characteristically there is misty weather with low stratus clouds, and no tendency to form cumulus clouds over the land.

A stable wind follows the coastline, increasing its speed in narrow sounds and changing direction as it passes over flat rocky islands. The air current is warmed by the heat of the sun rising from the rocks, and veers to the right. F94

a stable wind follows the coastline, accelerating in sounds and straits, and changing direction over flat rocky islands

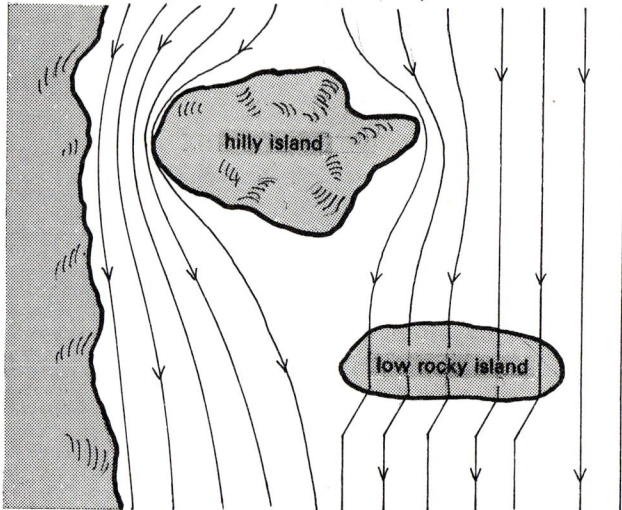

F94

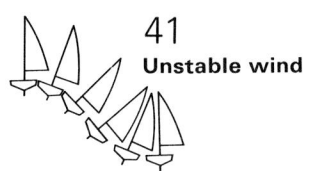

An unstable wind contains strong squalls from the isobar wind. It may deviate 10–15 degrees from the normal wind direction.

It is very important to determine the direction of these squalls when planning a race. You must be on the starboard tack when squalls strike from the right, and on the port tack when they come from the left, to get to the windward mark first.

Observation of squalls from an island, F95, F96
Take up your position on the highest point on the island and determine the wind direction with the aid of a compass. Take a bearing during a powerful squall and compare the direction with your first observation. Squalls are easy to spot on the water, and while they are blowing the wind indicator will move to the right or left. Hold your compass immediately under or in line with the wind indicator and read off the number of degrees of wind shift.

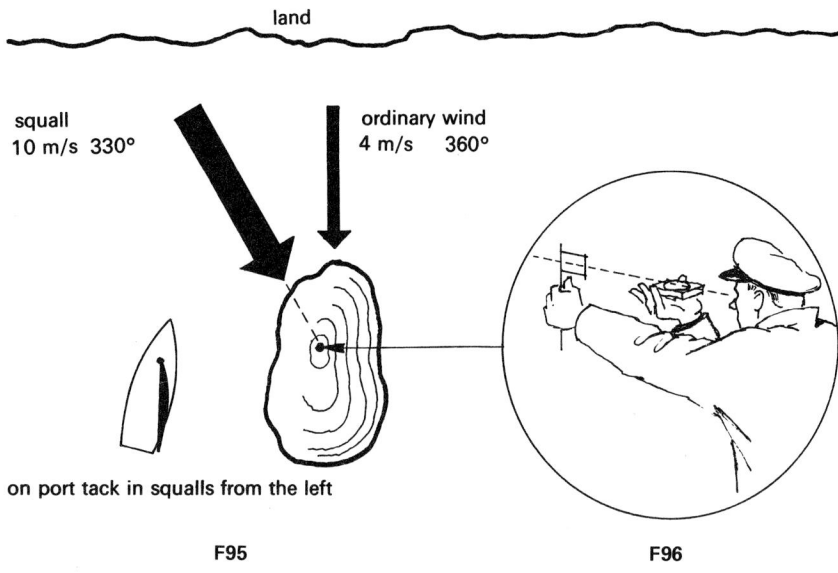

land

squall
10 m/s 330°

ordinary wind
4 m/s   360°

on port tack in squalls from the left

F95

F96

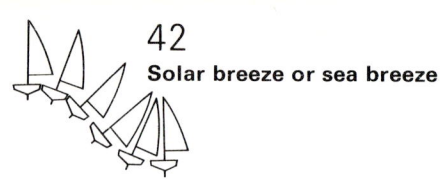

Solar breeze or sea breeze

The solar breeze is a local wind blowing onto the land from the sea and mixing with the winds we have already described. On warm, sunny days the solar breeze dominates, and most regattas are sailed in this sort of wind.

From about 8–10 a.m., when the land temperature starts to exceed the sea temperature, it is more or less calm. As the sun gradually warms the rocks and sandy beaches the temperature rises, and the sea wind blows at right angles to the coast (F97). It increases in strength, gradually veering clockwise and reaching maximum force around 3–6 p.m.

It falls light when the land mass starts to cool. The sea wind then backs anti-clockwise and dies out. During the evening and night, cold air from marshes and boggy ground moves across the land towards the higher temperature over the sea. This offshore wind continues to increase until just after sunrise. It then backs clockwise and finally blows with the land to the right in the morning. F98

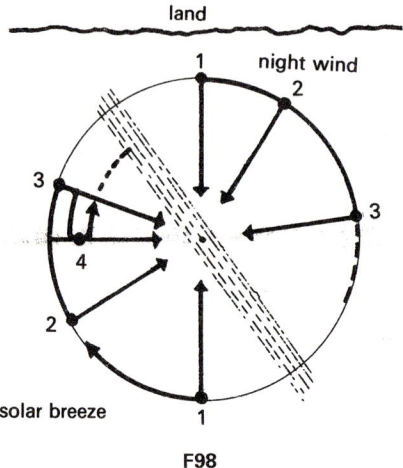

land

night wind

solar breeze

F98

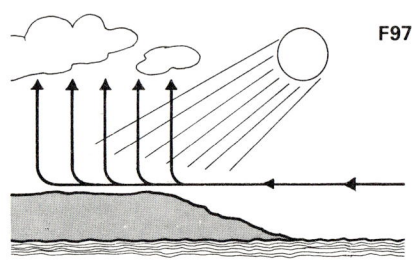

F97

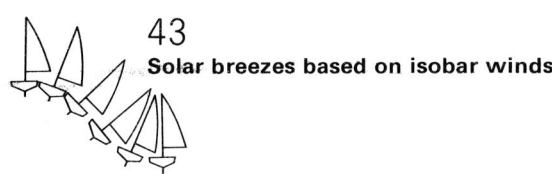

Solar breezes based on isobar winds

1 Determine the isobar wind at 8 a.m. Phone a met station and ask for the direction and strength of the wind up to 1000 metres, or release a balloon yourself and measure the direction of drift with a compass. P47

2 Plot the direction of the isobar wind.

3 Calculate the solar breeze on the basis of the following fundamental rules:

An isobar wind of 45 degrees blowing perpendicularly onto the coast veers and grows in strength in the course of the day.

An isobar wind of 180 degrees increases, backing.

An isobar wind of 225 degrees increases, backing.

An isobar wind of 270 degrees remains constant, only veering a little, with a possibility of increasing later in the day and blowing from the opposite direction. F99

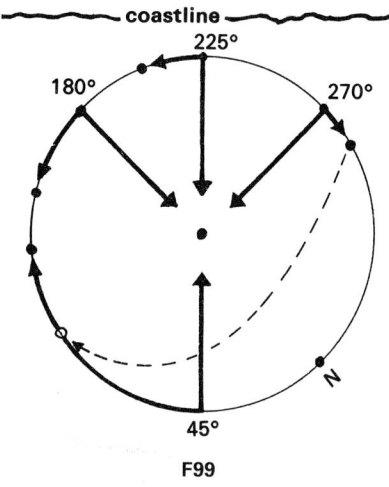

F99

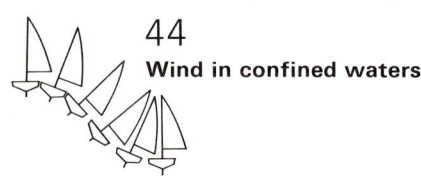

44
Wind in confined waters

The wind takes its direction from the land contours over which it blows. In most countries regattas are held in sheltered waters. For this reason, it is very important, in predicting the winds during a regatta, to study a detailed map of the surrounding country before racing starts. In addition, you should sail round the course in advance, taking compass bearings of wind and current.

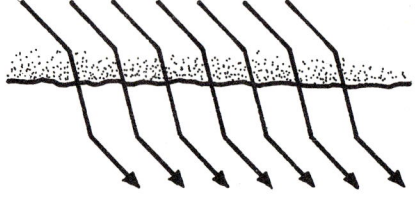

F101

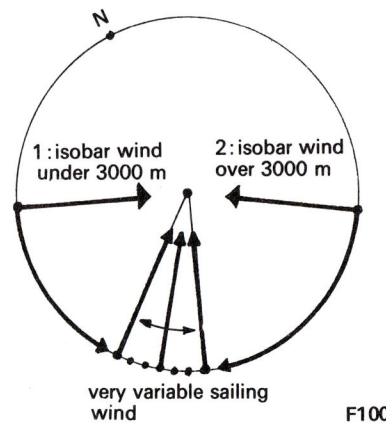

N

1 : isobar wind under 3000 m

2 : isobar wind over 3000 m

very variable sailing wind

F100

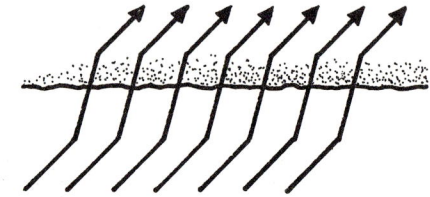

Solar breeze based on two isobar winds
Two isobar winds of different strength and direction blowing over the regatta course can make the solar breeze very tricky to sail in. For long periods at a time it may vary in direction and strength without any apparent reason. Knowledge of these two component isobar winds may be a help in forecasting a solar breeze of this kind. This was how the solar breeze behaved in Acapulco. F100

When the wind blows across a shoreline it changes direction. This should be borne in mind when the windward mark is situated just offshore. F101

P47

Jan Herman Linge, designer of the Soling, releasing a weather balloon in order to measure drift — the surest method of finding the direction of the wind

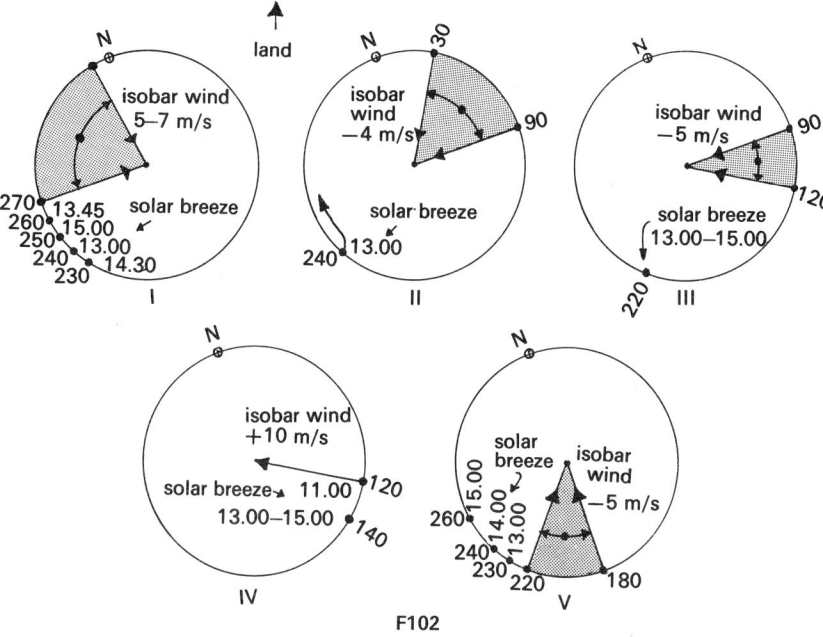

F102

With the aid of meteorological balloons we can discover the direction of the solar breeze (sea breeze) in unfamiliar waters. This is the wind pattern for the Olympic course at Acapulco in 1968, worked out by the author in October 1967 and 1968 for the Norwegian team. F102

The basis for the above observations is the direction and strength of the isobar wind at 7.30 a.m., at an altitude of up to 1000 metres, indicated in five different compass sectors.

45
Wind on lakes

It is very difficult to sail on lakes as the wind there behaves in a very special way. On calm days only the sun warming the surrounding land areas creates a wind. When the wind increases it veers, and when it falls off it backs. F103

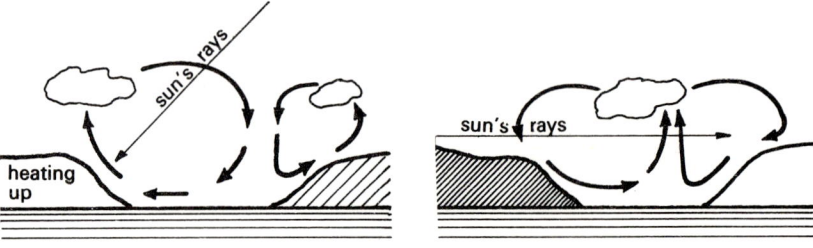

F103

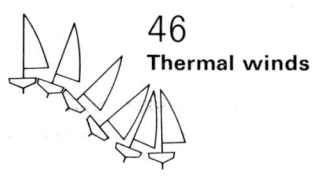

46
Thermal winds

This wind occurs in periods of complete calm. The sun warm the islands and fields in the vicinity, creating a wind as the hot air rises. Beaches and towns also absorb and are warmed by the rays of the sun, and there are nearly always thermals in their vicinity. The wind is stronger closer to land or islands. F104

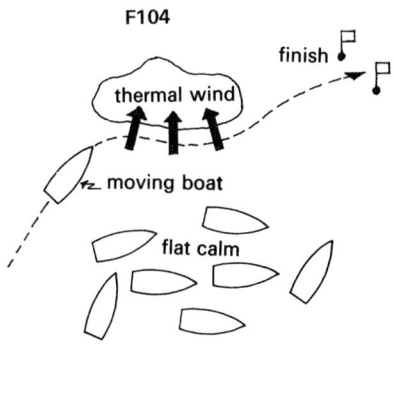

F104

finish

thermal wind

moving boat

flat calm

coastline

Some tips about wind

A rising wind veers (clockwise); a falling wind backs (anticlockwise).

High and low clouds drifting in the same direction mean unchanged wind conditions. A change in cloud formation foretells a change of wind.

Rising day temperatures make the wind veer more, and the wind strength will increase during the afternoon.

The wind will drop as it gets colder towards evening, and will back. When the morning wind blows from the NE off the south coast (with land on the right) there will be good weather, with a solar breeze. Conversely, a morning wind from the SW means blustery weather. When a wind accompanied by rain from low-lying cloud drops, the new wind will blow from a different direction.

In a thunderstorm the wind will first blow directly against the clouds, and then it will veer and blow away from the storm. Once the thunderstorm is over, the wind will probably veer.

When sun rays penetrate through a veil of fog or mist, the wind will increase and veer.

Dew in the morning means a nice bright day.

Dry grass in the morning means gusty weather with strong winds.

A wind backing = rain, and a wind veering = fine weather.

A rainbow to windward = rain, and to leeward = dry weather.

Insects settling on the deck are a warning of stormy weather.

When the ocean wind drops, sail further out from the coast. The wind will be stronger out at sea.

When the ocean wind drops on sunny days, sail close to the coast. Do not sail in the middle of the course.

Make for the open sea late in the evening.

There ocean breezes linger longest.

Weather sign for an abnormal wind with squalls from the left: strong wind from a clear sky.

Weather sign for a normal wind with squalls from the right: large cumulus (good weather) clouds over the land.

When sailing in a sea breeze: sail out to sea to meet it; sail in towards the coast when it drops.

Weather sign that the sea breeze will be blowing early in the day: large cumulus over the land and a weak night wind.

Weather sign that the sea breeze will be blowing late or coming up suddenly: warm and cloudless in the morning, or a dense layer of cloud that is quickly burnt up.

In an abnormal sea breeze with gusts of wind from the left, a wind shift will be accompanied by an increase in wind, probably from the left.

48
Strategy

The time just before a race is more important than the race itself. Information must be obtained which will provide the basis for correct strategy on the first windward leg.

You should aim to familiarise yourself with wind and current so as to avoid running into unexpected conditions during the race itself. Make wind and current observations, and plot these on the chart showing the course. Study depths, and mark the places where the current is most favourable; take a look at the country round about, and decide where the wind is liable to change direction, and make up your mind which tack will give you least wave resistance.

Start the day with a little light physical exercise, so that you can tone up, have a good meal, listen to the weather report, and be out on the course at least two hours before the starting time. Sail your boat aggressively and forget your rivals on the first windward leg. They'll know less about the conditions than you do.

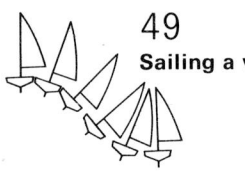

Sailing a winning course without a current

To windward
Sail in the direction of the general wind shift. Make four major tacks on the half of the course the wind shift is coming from, and make your last tack towards the mark from the same side as the wind shift and squalls.

Broad reaching
Bear away in the squalls, and luff up as the wind decreases. Your main course should lie well to leeward of the mark, enabling you to make your final spurt to the mark at full speed, pointing higher into the wind.

Close reaching
On the reaching leg the wind comes from ahead in squalls. This makes it possible to sail a faster course to windward of the straight line course all the way.

Running
Bear away in the squalls on a port tack and luff up when the wind falls light. Remain on the port tack the whole time.

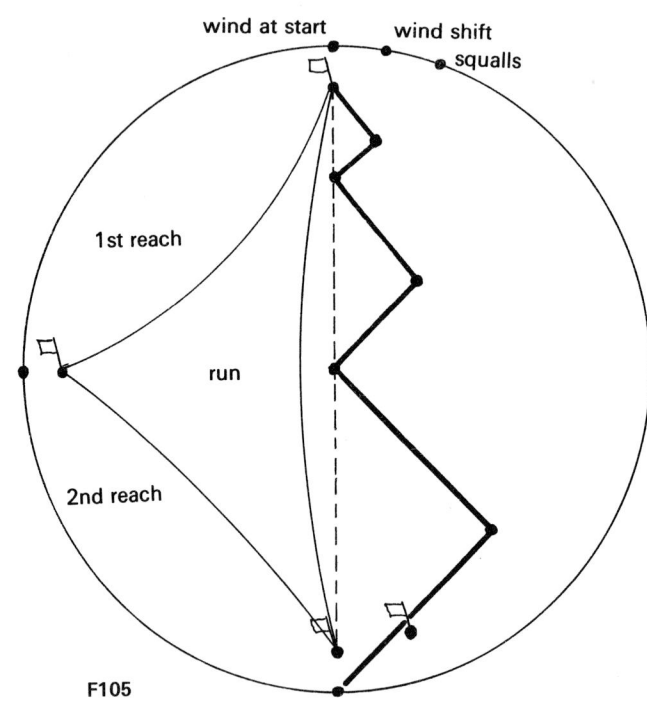

F105

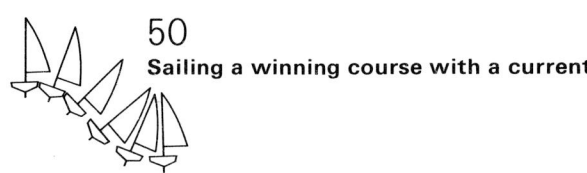

50
Sailing a winning course with a current

Beating: make all the use you can of the current. Sail on the tack that will bring your boat nearer to the windward mark. F76

Reaching and running: calculate the course you will steer in such a way that the leeway course between marks is a straight line. F106

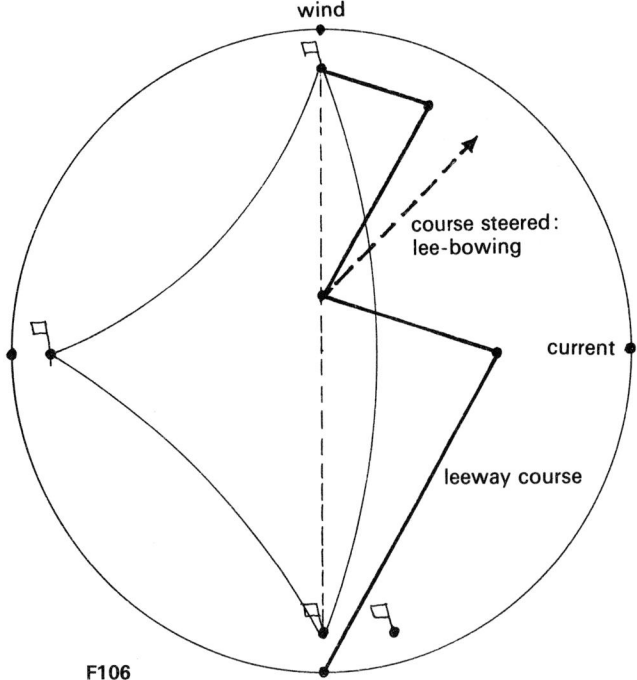

wind

course steered: lee-bowing

current

leeway course

F106

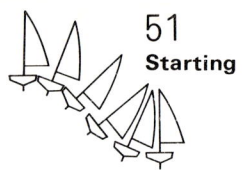
It is most important to start close to the windward mark, giving you a free wind after the starting gun. P48

It is very risky lying in the first rank waiting for the gun. It means that you are in a defensive position, and that rivals' manoeuvres will affect your next move. Per Werenskiold is probably the only one of our ace dinghy sailors who is a past master of this manoeuvre.

It is safer to sail aggressively in the second row, at full speed and in freer wind, with a chance of slipping into an opening on the starting line just before the gun. It is also much better to be in the second rank closest to the favoured end rather than to be in the first row on the wrong end of the starting line.

In smaller fleets of 30–50 boats it is essential to be close to the windward mark to have a chance of winning.

Per Werenskiold, N83, in one of his phenomenal starts in a fleet of over 100 Finn dinghies during the Kiel regatta, 1968

P48

![image]

If your plan involves sailing on the starboard half of the course, it pays to start close to the starboard mark, and to go onto the port tack at once.

Wind is diverted when it strikes a compact mass of sails on a starting line. It then pays to start on the outside. F107

When the wind blows at right angles to the starting line, it does not matter where you cross it. Even though the windward mark is not dead ahead, the distance to it will be the same for all boats beating up to the mark.

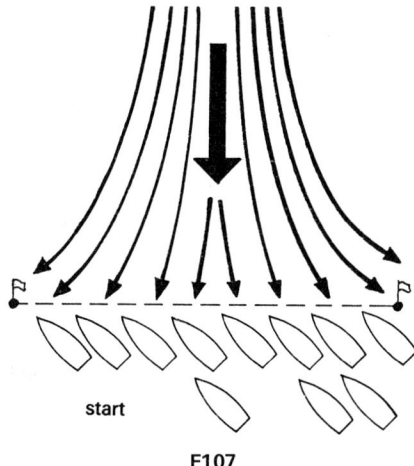

F107

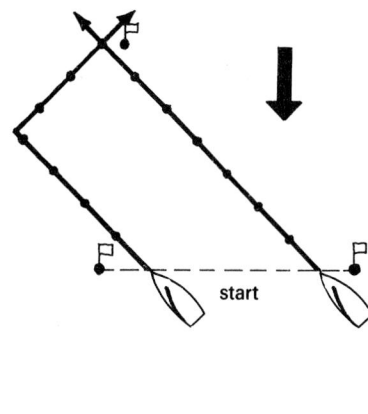

start

F108

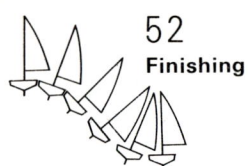

The finishing line is rarely at an angle of 90 degrees to the direction of the wind. The committee boat at the finishing line generally takes up her position by the mark closest to the wind, in order to get the boats to cross the line farther away, near the other mark, though this is not always so.

Your final approach to the finishing line should be made from the half of the course from which wind shifts or squalls will come, so that you get your last decisive lift from the wind just before crossing the finishing line. Always calculate the position of the boats when sailing to windward in relation to the

direction of the wind, and not according to their position in relation to one another. Just before the finishing line this is of very great importance.

The shortest course to the finishing line is close to the mark that is farthest to leeward. F110

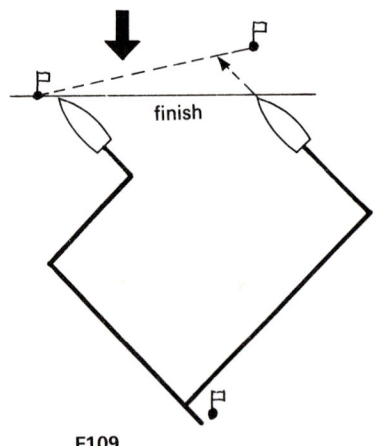

F109

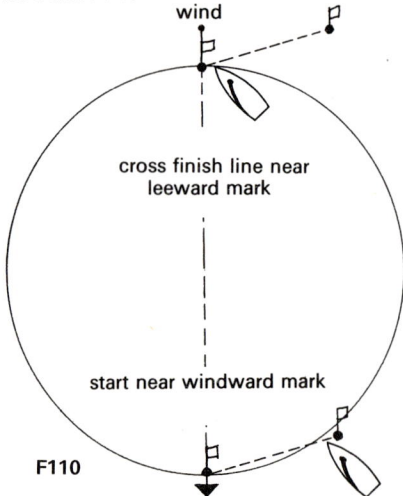

F110

P49

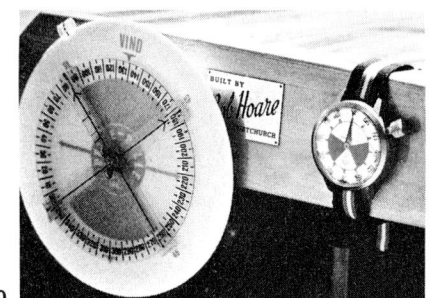

P50

A modern sailing compass and a bearing disc mounted on board the FD *Tine*

The compass is an essential aid for working out the best strategy and finding the marks, the direction of wind and current, and the position of the starting line on the modern triangular regatta course. P49

It is, of course, possible to manage without it, but that would mean basing decisions on guesswork and assumption, and that is not very satisfactory. In hazy or foggy conditions it might be impossible.

A small bearing disc is a useful aid for noting down and keeping observations when racing. One can, of course, also plot them in a compass rose, with the boat's position on the regatta course always assumed to be in the centre of the compass. P50, F111

On page 106 is a scheme for the first windward leg, based on observations made with a compass before starting. F111.

Direction and strength of wind:
Luff up dead into the wind. Hold the wind indicator in your hand above the compass and take a bearing of the direction of the wind, or make a short dead run with the pennant of the indicator between the arms, and read off the bearing. Mark 360 degrees on the compass rose on a sheet of paper, this being the true wind direction.

Hold a wind gauge up against the wind and read off the wind strength.

Direction and strength of current:
Drop a miniature current gauge or a small piece of paper, etc, from the starting buoy, then let it drift for 30 seconds. Take the bearing of its drift with a compass (55 degrees).

Boat's steered course:
Sail to windward with full sails, on starboard and then on port tack, and read off the courses from the compass. Note (for example) starboard 305 degrees, port 35 degrees. This tells us that the current is running against us on the port tack because we are pointing 10 degrees higher than normal.

compass observation made before the start and plotted on a compass rose

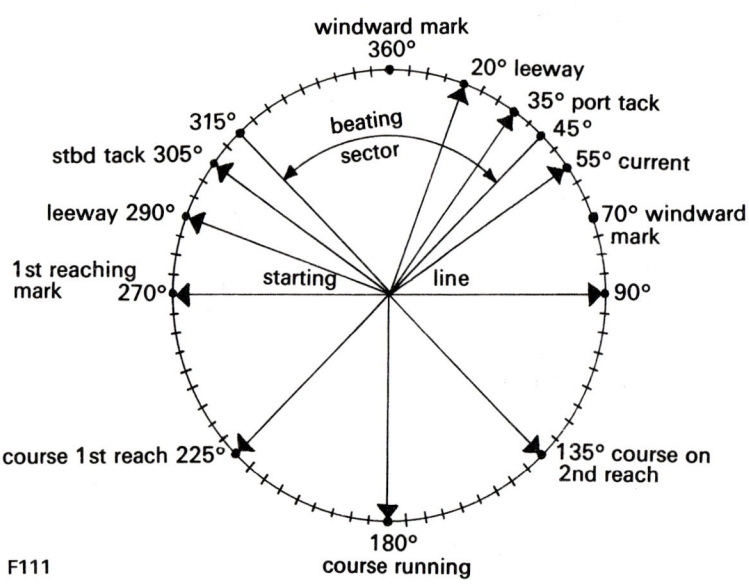

F111

The boat moves more slowly through the air and for this reason points higher.

Direction of drift:
Sail to windward for two minutes from the starting buoy on the previously observed courses for starboard and port tacks, then take a bearing of the starting buoy. Take the reciprocal of this bearing and note (for example) starboard 290 degrees, port 20 degrees. These observations are highly important as they will provide the basis for calculating the 'winning' course, and for deciding which half of the course should be selected if you are going to win. Port tack will take your boat nearer to windward mark, and for this reason we shall choose the starboard half of the course.

Starting line:
Start outside one of the marker flags and steer in such a way that the course you are sailing coincides with the line of sight between the marks. Take a bearing on this transit with your compass and note it down, 70 degrees. A starting line at right angles to the direction of the

wind would be 270 degrees to 90 degrees. A bearing of 70 degrees means that the starting line is 20 degrees out, and that the starboard mark is closest to the wind. A rough guide if you have no compass is to sail down the starting line with your sails correctly trimmed and cleated, and tack without altering sail trim. If the sails are then overtrimmed, the wind is freer on the new tack and this is the end at which to start.

Course to the windward mark:
This should be announced by the race committee, but this is not always done. The mark can be made conspicuous by a balloon, the bearing of which can easily be taken with a compass. Note 360 degrees.

Courses to the reaching and running marks:
Compass courses to the first and second

reaching marks are always placed at 45 degrees to the left and right of the starting mark, and the starting position in the compass rose is always the opposite of the wind direction. Note 225 degrees, 135 degrees and 180 degrees. F111

Race between two boats to determine the more advantageous half of the course. This is a very realistic test which, provided it gives the same result several times running, gives a very accurate picture of the prevailing wind. Both boats start off at the same time on opposite tacks from the same mark, sail for two minutes, come about and meet again. The boat in the lead has had the most favourable wind. F112

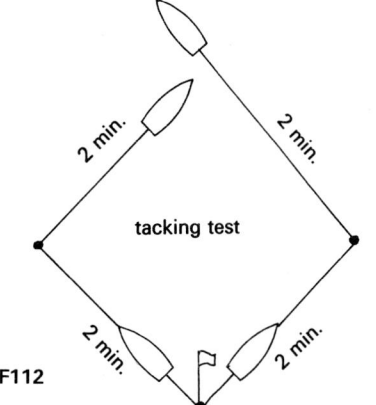

tacking test

2 min.

2 min.

2 min.

2 min.

F112

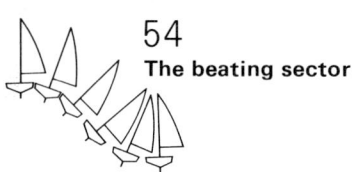

54
The beating sector

When two boats work their way up towards the windward mark from start to finish, the boat sailing a course which at all times is within a sector the sides of which subtend an angle of 45 degrees to the general direction of a wind, will win.

By sailing with reference to the oscillations continuously shown by the compass, the crew can check whether the boat's course lies within the beating sector. This is the most important task for the crew when sailing to windward. F113

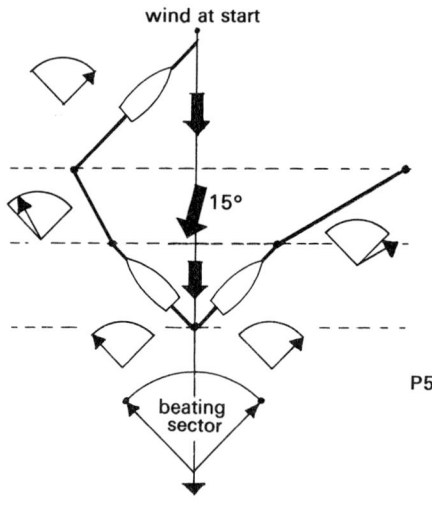

wind at start

15°

beating sector

F113

Tools and vacuum flask

Scale on boom for regulating the foot of the sail

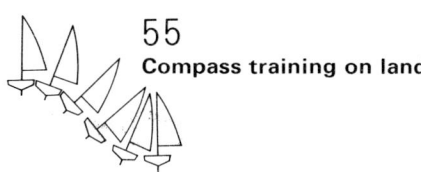

Compass training on land

This is excellent training in strategy. Pace out a miniature course on a field or lawn, on the basis of a compass rose, with marks, wind and current plotted in advance. Competitors should be given the speed of the current and the boats, for example 2 and 4 knots respectively, and they should be asked to walk up the *leeway courses* to windward with the aid of a compass. The instructor should start competitors off one by one, checking their courses with his compass and analysing each course in a discussion afterwards. P53

P53

Bjørn Lofterød, Norwegian FD helmsman, on a simulated compass windward leg, during a training session for the Olympic team in the autumn of 1968

Lay a windward leg with the windward mark close to land, so that a shift of wind occurs at the end of the beat.
Competitors: boats from various classes.
Object: to find the winning course to windward, and to sail on the faster half of the course.
Prepare and carry out a correct start.
Make four tacks and calculate the time to go about for the last beat.

Allow competitors to sail once round the course, so that they can take wind and current observations. After the race competitors should plot the tacks made on a training card. In a discussion afterwards the instructor should go through the race with each competitor.

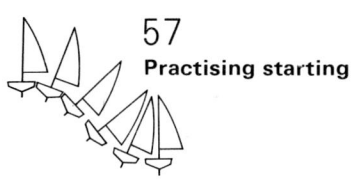

57
Practising starting

A good way of training helmsmen and crews in mass starts is to arrange races for a number of similar and differing classes of boats, such as the Flying Dutchman and the Trapeze, the Finn and the OK dinghy, the Enterprise, GP 14, Albacore, Fireball, Snipe, Soling and Squib, to mention a few. The main point is to ensure that as many boats as possible start. The angle of the starting line to the wind should be varied. Boats need not complete the windward leg, but should return to the starting line and make a fresh start. Afterwards the instructor can comment on the performances of the crews and helmsmen involved. In order to remember the sequence of events, it is a good idea to record comments at the time on a tape recorder, and if possible take photographs or video tapes.

P54

Lay a narrow channel dead to windward, using firmly anchored floats joined together with lines as markers, so that boats are compelled to go about every 20 or 30 seconds. Send the boats off one by one, and take the time required for sailing through with a stopwatch.

Excess heeling
Photo: Michael Richardson

59
Speed training with two boats

This is the most important training exercise. Participants should be paired off and each pair of boats should race, boat A against B, and so on.

1 Boat B trims her sails for top speed and takes up a position forward and to leeward, but without obstructing the other boat. Boat A chases boat B until boat A achieves a greater speed.

2 The boats change places. Continue until both boats sail faster.

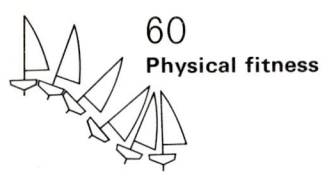

Danish and French dinghy sailors use an apparatus of the kind shown in F114, for conditioning the muscles used when sitting out. The rope runs through a block and is attached to a 10 kg weight to produce the effect of pulling at the sheet. The exercises are done in the following order. F115

1 Mark time with high knees.
2 Lean right back and pull at the 'sheet' with left and right arms alternately.
3 Sit down on the floor with your ankles wedged under a fixed object. Place both hands on your head with your elbows out to the side. Bend backwards and forwards, with your elbows touching the floor and the opposite knee alternately.
4 Adopt the normal sailing position on the apparatus, and pull at the sheet alternately with your left and right arm.
5 Stand with your arms stretched upwards above your head, then crouch and place your hands on the floor. Extend your body with all weight on hands and toes and the body straight.
6 Lean right back on the apparatus, carrying a weight on your chest.
7 Exercise 4.
8 Exercise 8.

Together with other forms of physical training, such as running, these exercises will help you to keep in the right condition during the winter season. Training together as a group, under the eye of an instructor, who will see to it that the other joints and muscles in your body are also kept up to scratch, is a good idea. Check your pulse rate at regular intervals, to see what sort of shape you are in. The lower it is, the better.

F114

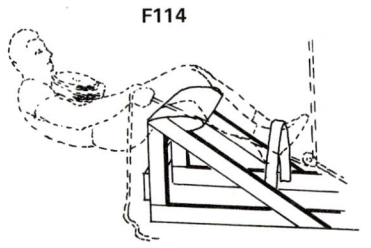

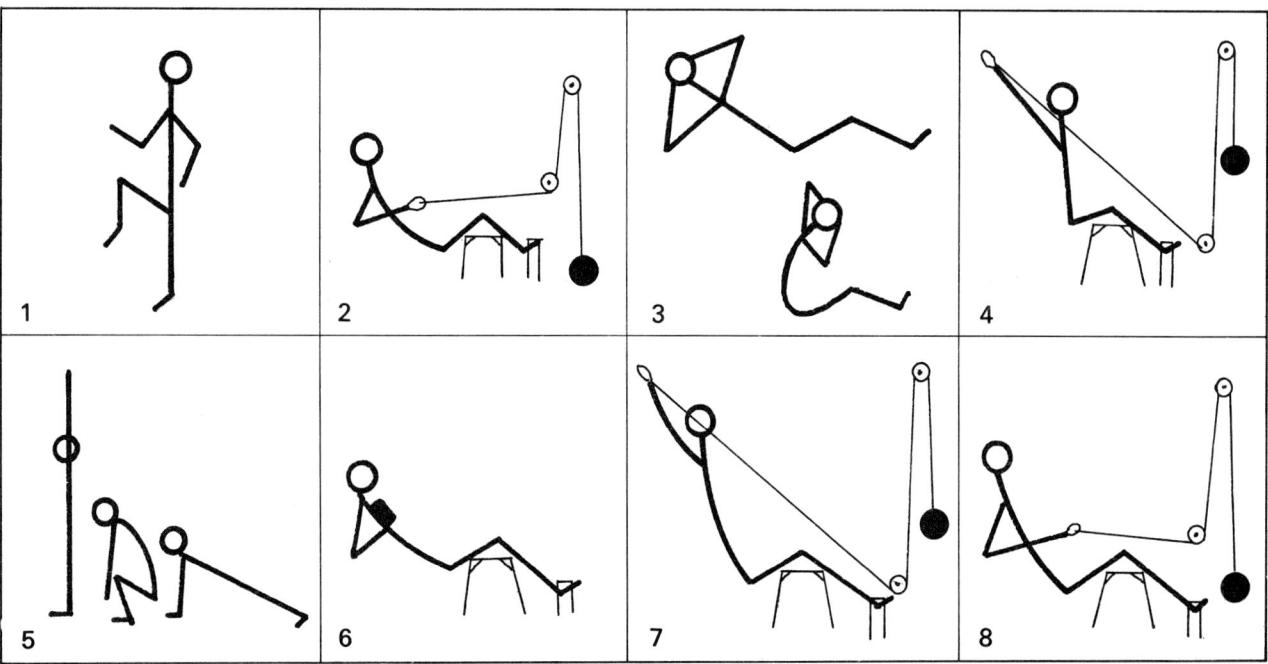

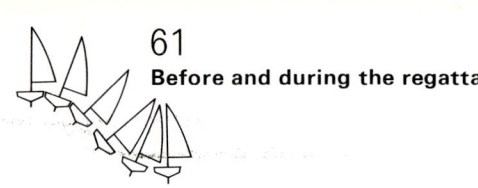

Experience proves that it is an advantage to turn up for a series of races as early as possible. A long period of adjustment to local conditions is very important.

There are various points that should be run through before you are prepared to start.

You have already achieved peak physical condition through intense training. It is now too late to do anything about this aspect of sailing. It is on the psychological plane that the winning helmsman will make his mark. When the starting gun goes, the need for non-sailing amusements, such as seeing the local sights, should have been satisfied, and a state of perfect concentration must be achieved. A championship series lasts more than a week. The will to win must increase with every day, culminating in the race on the final day. There will not be room for anything but sailing, if peak form is to be achieved in the last race.

For this reason it is an advantage for the sailor to shun all other kinds of recreation so that he can concentrate entirely on racing. Up early in the morning, off for a day's racing and plenty of sleep at night should be the daily routine.

P55
Sailing in
heavy swell

During a series of races the body is under considerable pressure. In the last resort this may undermine the ability to make the right decision. To avoid this, an 'instant' lunch that will act quickly as a tonic should be carried on board. This boat lunch, enough for one person, was used by leading Norwegian helmsmen and crew with excellent results during the Olympic Games in 1968.

Mix
25 g non-fat dry milk powder
30 g malted milk powder
50 g sugar
20 g corn oil
200 g fresh water
Pour the mixture into a plastic bottle and drink just before the start of your race. This mixture contains sugar, protein and fat, and will keep you mentally and physically alert.

Glucose or blackcurrant juice are excellent during racing.

For breakfast: orange juice, milk, tea with plenty of sugar, bacon and eggs, bread and jam, honey or marmalade. Avoid drinking too much; instead, drink orange juice at hourly intervals before the start of your race. This diet is enough for one daily ration. As a general rule you won't feel the pangs of hunger until later in the evening.

For dinner: be careful what you eat, especially when you are abroad. Meat well done and fresh fish should be a sufficient diet. Milk, too, should be drunk. Fruit, peeled, is an important source of vitamins.

The following simple remedies are recommended:
For seasickness—Quells, Sealegs or other proprietary brands. Use one which you know from experience works for you, and take it well before going on the water.
For headaches, general aches and pains—paracetamol, codeine, aspirin. Aspirin can be a stomach irritant.
For skin rashes—calamine lotion.
For sore throat —Dequadin or other proprietary lozenges.
For diarrhoea—kaolin and morph., Chlorodyne, Lomotil (on prescription).
For sleeplessness—sleeping pills as prescribed by your doctor, of a type which you have already tried. Alcohol taken with or after sedatives may potentiate the effects, causing oversleeping or dopiness the next day.
To prevent ill effects of heat, sunlight and glare, wear white clothes and sunglasses.

63
Winning course card

winning course card no.

race

date

boat   crew

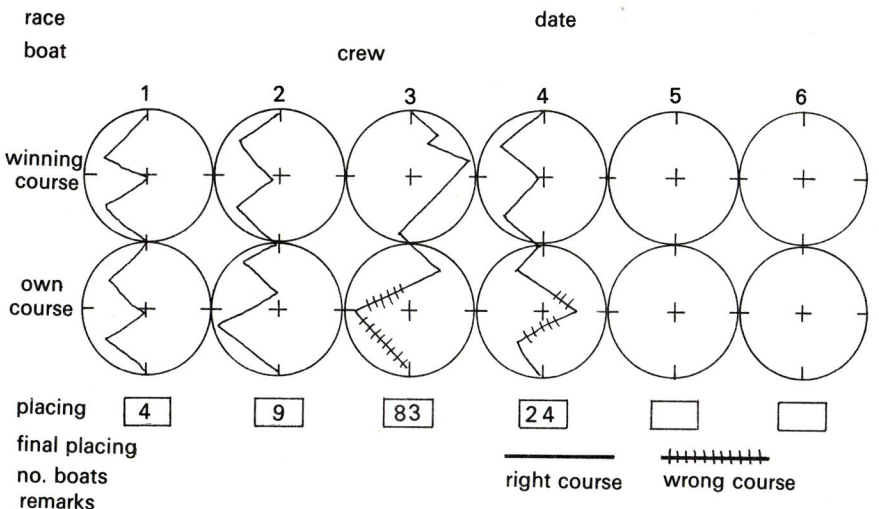

	1	2	3	4	5	6
winning course						
own course						
placing	4	9	83	24		
final placing						
no. boats						
remarks						

right course ——————   wrong course +++++++++

F116

119